Messages from Spirit

By Irene Martinez

Copyright © 2024

ISBN: 978-1-9999220-5-4

First Edition

Acknowledgements

I would like to thank my son Jose for his help in getting this book finalised and supporting me throughout the creation of this book, which I couldn't have achieved alone.

In memory of Canon John Barnes who was there at the beginning of my story who supported and helped me over the years.

Contents

1. A Spiritual Journey — 8
2. Trials of Temptations — 10
3. Repentance — 12
4. Climate Change — 13
5. The Afterlife — 15
6. Treasures of Life — 17
7. Faith and Wisdom — 18
8. Storms of Life — 20
9. Anchor for Life — 22
10. God's Plans — 24
11. Good Friday — 26
12. Crucifixion — 29
13. Celebrate Easter — 31
14. Understanding Life — 33
15. God's Garden — 35
16. Parable Teaching — 38
17. Temptations — 40
18. Alpha and Omega of Life — 42
19. Powers of Contact — 43
20. God Rules — 45
21. Vision of Life — 47

22. Parables Transformed to Gospels	49
23. Shores of Knowledge	51
24. Seasons of Life	53
25. Realms of Darkness	56
26. God Doesn't Want Suffering	58
27. Stand Firmly on the Rock	61
28. Seashores of Life	62
29. The Universe	64
30. Your Never Solitary	66
31. The Christ Child	68
32. Christmas Message	70
33. Are Prayers Heard?	72
34. Key to Illness	74
35. Life's Journey on Earth	76
36. My Visions	77
37. Author's View of Good and Evil	80
38. Life's Laws	82
39. God chooses Messengers	85
40. Guidance	87
41. Life Journey	88
42. God's Solutions	89
43. Be an Example	90
44. Path of Salvation	92

45. I'm here to Help	95
46. Healing and Suffering	97
47. Be the Image of Christ	98
48. How the Messages and Teachings Came	100
49. God's Intervention	102
50. Discuss God Freely	103
51. Plants in the Garden of Life	106
52. The Spirits Journey with Irene	108
53. Recollections of My Story	112

Introduction

It took many years of suffering before I decided to write my first book, *Trials, Torments, and Teachings*. This is my second spiritual book, written through the power of the Holy Spirit and my sensitivity to visions. These visions enabled me to convey messages from the wisdom of God to help people live their everyday lives better.

Since the mid-1980s in Turkey, I've faced constant attacks from demonic strongholds for being a Christian. Initially, I did not realize that I was sensitive and mediumistic. I have documented the full account of my true story in another book titled *Haunted by Demons: The Irene Martinez Story*. When this strange, paranormal nightmare began, I was working in show business in Turkey with one of my variety shows. I had been in show business from a young age, trained as a performer and all-round entertainer, unaware that I had the gift of sensitivity, which allowed me to hear spirits and see visions when this condition entered my life.

Everything I've written comes from my personal experience of living as a sensitive, which has caused significant illness and suffering in my everyday life. The stigma from Turkey has left lasting effects on my health and well-being to this day. This condition creates hellish, devastating effects for a victim to cope with, due to paranormal attacks by strongholds of evil spirits. My book, *Haunted by Demons: The Irene Martinez Story*, provides a realistic look into this condition and explains what many people might be suffering from, often unaware of what is truly happening to them during these sadistic attacks.

As a Christian who has suffered with this condition for half of my life, as mentioned in the Bible, I have remained faithful to Christianity. This faithfulness is why I was given the messages and have the capability to write them down. These words, coming from the Spirit, are a gift of wisdom and knowledge to pass on to people through this book. It shows that God's power is endless and can easily reach the world through people like myself who have the gift to do this work. After years of battling the powers of darkness and enduring near-death experiences, I have soldiered on.

So, I hope everyone who reads this book will gain some knowledge from the messages. May God bless you and keep you safe from the wiles of the enemy in your life, and home. Let the messages become a valuable tool you can turn to and use throughout your life. To pass onto future generations

Irene is a close friend of mine with whom I can easily connect. She's my equal, and we both loathe the enemy. She is working on this assignment with me for the Christian faith. Irene has earned her diploma as a worthy Christian soldier.

As a Christian, your battle with the enemy has raged on endlessly over the years, and I admire your courage. This is because you were given the power of the Spirit to do the Lord's work on earth, using the messages in this book to spread the word of God.

1
A Spiritual Journey

Stop, and feel the stillness of life as it covers and protects you. Believe in the one who created all living things on earth, including each individual person born with a purpose from God. Although weeds can grow and cover a person's path during their lifetime, making life's journey harder to bear without guidance. So, we call for the gardener who plants all living things in the world to clear the overgrowth from our lives, making our journey less hazardous.

Never doubt His ways. He accepted the burden of the tree to instil new hope for life after the death of the body. The resurrection brought thoughts of a life after death in God's kingdom, where there is peace and divine love for the Christian believers who follow in His footsteps with joyful hearts.

Various teachings which I have given Irene can be used in your everyday lives. She is one of the few people who can interpret what I mean and understands my way of giving messages through parables. Being a natural sensitive, she is able to receive my words and write the messages, which I hope will be spread through this book and various talks in churches that follow Christianity.

Irene has persevered to write my words correctly with great patience for this book. She warns people from her own experience of living daily with the enemy and strongholds of unclean spirits interfering in her life for many years. This is a life-threatening experience for anyone to live through, giving her a great deal of firsthand knowledge of how the enemy enters into people's lives and gains residence.

Although many battles have taken place in her life with the realms of darkness over the years, she has developed into a Christian soldier who has marched on endlessly in God's glory as an example. This is why people should read her books to appreciate the truth she has written from her own experience of living between two worlds. Her experiences prove the truth of many stories written in the Gospels, along with her other book, "Haunted by Demons: The Irene Martinez Story." This book is a good documentation of what she has endured as a Christian. My peace be with you, Irene, and your group, and my people around the world.

Proverb for us both

We know the enemy exists in the world as we've experienced his vial of poison, and refused to take it.

2
Trials of Temptations

You are my shield and armour of defence, my sword in times of trouble to defend me. I bow before you and turn to you in my darkest hour with a sincere heart, to be healed by the living God.

Open your eyes and see the wonders of the planet that are around you. Take time to gaze at creation that's everywhere and enjoy it. I'm thankful for the people who remain faithful to the word without ceasing, who follow in my footsteps during their lifetime on earth.

There are too many people in the world suffering from ill health, which isn't alleviated quickly. Various others are waiting to be delivered from long-term ailments. Also, a variety of strange supernatural forces are at work in the world, holding people captive. If you read the gospels, you'll see demons and unclean spirits were being cast out by Jesus. Well, those spirits are still around and active in the world today, still looking for victims to use as hosts, and people around the world are still being used by unclean spirits, waiting to be set free by the Lord's power.

Do you believe this is still going on, and did Jesus cast out unclean spirits like the gospels say? It's true and still happening; remember my words. What Irene is writing is my testimony too. The father of lies exists and is working overtime with his retinue from hell to create havoc in the world. Battles with the world of darkness can rage on for years and be ended by the power of God, which brings salvation to the body and soul. This power is able to reach out and touch the hearts of men and women alike, who are searching for peace from the Lord.

The trials of one's life can take place through error or injustice on the road we each travel on during our lifetime on earth. Another question often heard is, 'Are prayers heard?' As each person waits for their prayer to be answered to end whatever their suffering or trials they are going through, courage is needed to endure spiritual trials during one's lifetime on earth. Does the enemy cause any trials for the human race, or are we at fault for not being responsible or taking the wrong action when we change the rules we live by? Each person's life is full of unanswered questions.

Be vigilant, my people, with whom you mix, as the devil comes in various disguises. It could be anyone you come into contact with in your life, in the form of a woman or man who loves a life without limits, rules, or regulations, who encourages you to do the same. If this is the case, open your eyes and see where that friendship is leading. Be safe, my people, also vigilant against the snares of the enemy, who was once an angel.

3
Repentance

My love is endless like a father for his people, who through foolishness might have sinned. If this is the case, repentance is needed to gain forgiveness from God, who is merciful and wants his people to be set free from every type of oppression or bondage from past sins that one might be holding onto. So, you can experience freedom and peace in your entire body. If you follow what I say, you are on the right path to gaining the benefits of repentance, which you can then explain to other people who might be trapped by past sins they are still carrying.

This might create a deeper understanding for a person who might be filled with hatred and aggression through habitual sinning. My messages are being sent to you with the help of Irene so they can be used and passed on to other people who wish to learn my way of teaching. I hope my words instil a deeper faith in you and a greater understanding of God's love. Increase your faith when you pray, as the Lord waits for your prayers.

I am like a father who never abandons you. Remember this always, even if you have committed a multitude of misdemeanours through leading a wayward existence. I repeat, repent and gain forgiveness from God. It is the only way to become totally liberated, healed, and made whole again. Once we admit our sins, which we all commit from time to time as humans, God understands, forgives, and can heal you with His power. Have faith, trust Him, and it will come to pass.

Have a blessed day with my peace.

4
Climate change

For the human race to survive on planet Earth, it needs water, sunlight, and a stable climate to reap a plentiful harvest. Therefore, the planet must be treated with respect by the human race as it is crumbling away. The stream of life flows on through the shores of time, in a never-ending dimension from the past to the present.

God has kept the stream of human creation gracefully flowing on, despite wars brought about by mankind to destroy themselves and the world. Throughout all these disasters, the Earth's natural environment has continued evolving. Let's stop and think about what happens: floods, hurricanes, and eruptive volcanoes damage and burn the Earth dry. Droughts form cracks in the Earth's core, creating destruction for the planet. These disasters are not created by mankind and cannot be controlled or stopped by the human race.

The Creator hears the Earth's desperate cries and sends torrential rain from above to cool the charred Earth that moans in despair. As it cannot produce crops to sustain mankind, there is famine, disease, and suffering, with many people dying due to the shortage of food. Seeds and plants are unable to grow. Yet, the human race survives in the never-ending stream of life, which continues throughout the ages.

Christians pray for the second coming of Christ to teach modern civilization a way to enrich their lives and to be aware of what mankind creates to make life easier with various inventions that might eventually help destroy the Earth. Could a few simple words teach us how to lead better lives and how to be vigilant in taking care of the environment in the world that was created for us to live in by God? Would His words help, and do countries around the world understand the importance of working together to keep the natural environment intact and thriving, instead of dying through man's modern technology and devices? Some modern inventions create poisonous gases that can actually kill the planet over time, which was created with living streams of water to sustain life to the highest degree.

5
The After Life

Does a person's life end when they die? Let's discuss this theory. There's a lot written about people who've had near-death experiences. These people claim to have been in heaven. Some say they've seen God. So, is there an afterlife after death and the grave? Let me answer that question more clearly, through my way of thinking. There is another realm beyond the world we exist in, after our death on earth. Your views on this subject could differ from mine; you don't have to agree with me, and you can have your own opinion.

Many people say they've passed through the valley of the shadow of death and lived, finding the whole experience mind-shattering. They find out that another world does exist beyond the light, which gives people who fear death a pillar of hope. This hope can lessen the fear of the shadow of death when it approaches, as one's life comes to its earthly end.

My people, begin by letting go of the past and forgiving those who've hurt you. Allow yourself to do this so my light can flow freely into your bodies, healing and clearing the bondages holding you from the past. Allow the Lord to provide a better future for you. Negative things do take place in our lives, sometimes instigated by the enemy, for which God often gets the blame from the human race.

Irene, may your path be filled with light, along with the paths of other people who need light in their lives too. Treasures await those who put their trust in the father. Read King David's words in the Psalms and let them guide you in praising God abundantly. Pray for guidance, my people, and allow God to do the rest for you to understand His will. Contemplation and prayer will help you find ways of doing the Lord's work on earth for the few chosen people. Explain my messages to people the way I'm giving them to you. This will enable them to follow Christ's guidance and enlighten the universe with His wisdom. We all need to learn certain lessons in life, as Christ did when he was called by the Father to proclaim the Word, so the Gospels could be born and spread throughout the world.

People need freedom of thought, not enslavement by religious laws, but by finding the truth in God's words. Keep prayers and faith in your life, and in the Lord, throughout the darkest storms of your lives, and He will calm the turbulence, turning life's storms into a whisper.

The Lamb

6
Treasures of life

Wanting more than you need isn't bad; in fact, it can be an asset in learning to help other people who have fewer worldly assets. However, be aware of not becoming too greedy for material things in life and craving more than you need. The poorest people can teach the wealthy a lesson about life. For them, everyday things which have value are simple, like having enough food for the next meal and sufficient money to survive. These things are treasures for the poor, equal to a rich man's treasure.

It's not a crime to be wealthy if used wisely, or to learn to be generous to others who are less fortunate in life. This is a worthy lesson to learn from my messages. Having a person you can turn to in times of trouble, a good friend who's always there for you, is a treasure. Good health is a mountain of wealth given by the Lord to people. Love and being loved by another person in return is equal to a sack of gold. Along with the wonders of nature that we see all around us, these are treasures from God.

The birth of a child to a family is a blessing with the creation of a new life. Also, when sickness is restored to health in a person, it is a blessing. Every day, the human race receives a multitude of gifts, many unseen and all valuable treasures, which are not publicized in the media but are provided by the Lord and often go unappreciated.

God provides a multitude of wondrous things and never abandons His people from their birth to the end of their journey on earth. All we have to do is give thanks when we pray to the Lord, who provides so many treasures in the world we live in.

7
Faith & Wisdom

Praise the Lord, who suffered death's sting and was resurrected through the glory of the Father. He abides forever, shedding endless healing on the sick, poor, needy, and those living with despairing ailments. God's love is endless, penetrating the universe and filling it with faith, hope, and love, through the shores of time.

The hoofed one brings destruction and despair to the human race, so pray in Jesus's name for people to be healed, blessed, and set free from their trials of suffering. And, for members of your group and yourself, as millions of people throughout the world are terminally ill with infirmities of various types, pray for these people nonstop. God loves you and is your friend, who knows every breath you've taken since your birth. Life is precious, given by God, and equal to gold and silver.

When tears are shed, they're pearls from life's living oceans, from the stream of life. Lay not your hands upon things that will harm you, but do what's pleasing to God, who is the head of the church, not of people who deceive God's laws. Let faith guide your path to help needy people who wish to be followers of Christ.

Never fear people who follow the church's laws that are not in the manner Jesus taught them; these people will never be close to him. The gospels he preached became the New Testament, which has also been altered various times as the gospels were passed down over the centuries and rewritten. Trust in the messages that I give you with my words; they are truthful and filled with wisdom for you to interpret. You're a sensitive person who has the gift to write and spread the messages for me on earth at this time. Through your understanding and ability to recognize what I say, and your ability to write the messages, be strong and stand firm on the rock that I'll build for you. No more is needed than a sound heart that lives in his, who holds you up in times of trouble, as I'm close to each one of my people. Like a father you can depend on and trust, who helps you deal with life's trials, which everyone experiences during their lifetime on earth.

At night before you sleep, pray and think of me, as my journey on earth was a weary one many times, and the Father held me up during those times for the word of God to be born. Brothers and sisters from around the world, speak God's words daily to your children in a simple way. With an understanding and knowledge of the gospel stories, allow children to develop in the light and grow from small seeds into wondrous plants of intelligence and faith that can bear abundant fruit throughout their lifetime on earth.

End of teaching

8
Storms of life

Be merciful to other people; forgive them if they hurt you or the ones you love. See yourself needing mercy from others on your journey through life, as life can be tossed like the sea in a storm. Rough waves may cover your world, turning it into a sea of turbulence.

All situations and worries pass with time, enabling you to cope with the storms of life. This helps prevent you from being swept along by waves of doubt that you experience. The hazards of life will always continue to toss and turn throughout your earthly existence, but you can learn to face the storms and control them, or be drowned by them overwhelming you.

Keep your head above life's waves until the storm calms, and the waves reach the shore of life, leaving your footprints in the sands of time. See them in the sand before the incoming tide washes your footprints back into the sea, where they'll be swept to other shores by the changing tides of time, which sweep the oceans and seashores clean. When the storm calms, the wind turns into a whisper over the waves with the incoming tide.

This is a parable to meditate on when you're faced with life's perils that confront each one of us. There will always be storms erupting in our lives, instigated by the enemy to people or through our own misjudgement. To survive safely on our journey from beginning to end, we may never realize that the Lord was always there, clearing our path with every step we took, watching over us.

Have faith in the Lord's goodness and mercy. He is the Shepherd of His flock, whatever race, age, or creed you are. Let Him feed you the bread of life that you need for your bodies and souls to endure this life. Bathe in the glory of God's love, with the gift of eternal life from the Creator whose power created the world. So, when you take the body and blood, give thanks unto Christ.

Allow Him to be your strength, have hope in the renewal of faith. My people, remain in the light for your wellbeing to improve your health issues. Do things which are pleasing to God and see the wonderful rewards He can create for you.

9
Anchor for life

Roses have thorns, so treasure the graces you've been given in the world and enjoy them. Our Lady was steadfast in her nature, and Christ showed mercy and healing to people who were suffering. So, justice will be given to people who follow God's laws. Unto them shall be given the acts of the wise, so abide by the laws which were written on the tablets.

The Lord listens to all who call upon Him and will deliver you all from the perils that impound your lives, which might originate from the father of lies who still roams the earth with principalities and strongholds, who continue their war against God's people.

Jesus overcame the devil and all he offered, as He knew the outcome. The enemy's domain is one built of vices, corruption, and despair, leading to thoughts of death for those tempted to follow that path of destruction.

The Lord is an anchor to renew your life after the enemy's treachery has taken place. He brings hope and light back into your lives with new things, which will bring peace and happiness back to your lives. May my peace be with you all, with a multitude of joy each day. Trust in God's mercy that is sent daily to people in the world.

Christians are used as scapegoats and targets to attack in different ways by the enemy, with campaigns of war that still rage on to destroy God by attacking people with unclean spirits and demons. These types of retinues and strongholds are at work non-stop, twenty-four hours a day, to destroy people on earth. While God remains watchful over His flock until the raging storm has passed.

None of my people are alone in their suffering; I'm with you throughout the trials you encounter on your journey through life on earth.

I'm sure many of you are aware of what reversed your life into a hell state over the past years. Now is the time to reverse your life and start to pray for protection in your homes, bodies, and lives daily. Blessings and peace to you all, and to Irene for being my light, which enables me to send my messages through her to write on my behalf.

May the dove of peace rest on you all

10
Gods Plans

With Jesus' baptism in the river Jordan by John, He received the Holy Spirit. With the dove's descent upon Jesus, proclaiming Him the living God on earth, He was revealed as the chosen one to alter the course of history through Christianity. This marked the beginning of Jesus' ministry and gospel teachings, which gradually began to spread throughout the area. After His death, His disciples travelled and spread the gospels to various countries, although many of the original teachings were changed over time.

The cross was my ransom for mankind, with my death and resurrection into heaven serving as a sign for people to believe in God's power. Saying my name can change your life. Don't let fear or doubt cloud your judgment and take you away from me, my faithful followers.

Let me be an ocean of strength and a source of power for you all to draw from. If you're suffering from trials or bondages in your lives, whether mental or physical ailments, have faith they can be taken away over time. Trust me. Find time each day to pray to me, as your lives are closely intertwined with mine.

I want people to be set free whose lives are ruled by sin or have corruptive vices through the enemy's intervention. Let my healing light come down on everyone who is suffering, in body, mind, or spirit, to be healed in Jesus' name.

Reading the message which Irene has written for me will bring us closer together, and her words will help you find peace. Remember, both powers of good and evil are at work in the world twenty-four hours a day. From the advocate of evil from the realms of darkness, while God's kingdom is helping people to renew their health and lives. Meditation and silence are cleansing for the body and soul. So, allow yourself time to be still, and you'll find the answers to many of your problems that are bothering you.

Irene thinks, "Who am I?" With our inner connection, I reply, "I'm the light of the world for those who believe in me." Irene replies by thought, "Do you claim to be Jesus Christ?" "I am, for those who believe in me."

The Light

11
Good Friday

On Good Friday, blood flowed from the thorns that pierced Jesus' head as he was taken back to the Father. His journey of agony began to the hill of Golgotha. Surging pains tore through his body as he picked up the cross and bore the weight of the tree across his shoulders and back. Surging pains coursed through his body as he walked towards the hill of Calvary. With the tree growing heavier with each step he took, down that sun-drenched path to his destiny, which was written.

The weight of the tree left purplish imprints on his body, which was cut and bleeding profusely with every step he took on that journey of pain, as a ransom for mankind. He struggled on under the weight of the cross, with a tormenting, jeering crowd following him. To accomplish his destiny and be crucified on the hill of the skull, our Lady walked beside him like an inextinguishable light, her grief far beyond his own. Heart-rending tears flowed down her beautiful face from the everlasting love she felt for her son, with thoughts of his trials of agony that awaited him when swords would pierce both hearts.

The surging sun and intense heat beat down on his broken body, transforming the scene into one of tears, blood, and sorrow, mixing together with the heat of the sun rising from the ground. Staggering on, he leaned forward under the weight of the cross, his hair damp with sweat and blood, dripping down from the thorns onto his face. Depleted of energy, sweat dripped from his body as he walked on, bearing the weight of the tree with perseverance. Insults and abuse were hurled at him, with cries of, 'Save yourself if you can,' as he ascended the sun-drenched path to Golgotha.

Stones pierced his cut feet, leaving an everlasting trail of bloody footprints on the hill of the skull. Unbearable pains surged through his body from the indentations of the cross. Stumbling, he fell for the first time under the weight of the tree. It was lifted, and so was the whip. The tree grew heavier, engulfing him with its pressure for the atonement of sins he must bear. The time had come to fulfil his inevitable destiny from birth: to be crucified on the hill of Golgotha.

On arrival, his garments were torn from him, and he cried out in pain. The thorns shed sorrowful tears of blood down his forehead, face, and torso. His appearance was unrecognizable under the blazing rays of the sun, as the lamb went to the slaughter on the cross. A translucent halo of light surrounded him as he held onto the light of the world in oppressive heat. The light became more radiant as Jesus was nailed to the cross and hung there to die, solitary. Rays of white light emerged, surrounding the three crosses silhouetted against the sky.

Darkness covered the sky, thunder roared, and tears fell from heaven, pounding the ground that wept with sorrow. He endured the agony, as pain overwhelmed his body and soul for mankind. "Eloi, Eloi, God." Thunder roared, the sky opened, and rain lashed down onto the crowd that followed him to the hill. In semi-darkness, that moment was captured in time, together with the radiant light that surrounded the crosses, standing boldly against the dark sky. Blood flowed, and lightning struck the tree, where the lamb hung dying on its branches, tormented and abused, remaining silent throughout.

In darkness, the crowd who tormented him waited, as tears of rain fell from above and mixed with the Nazarene's blood as he died. A golden light encircled him as a sign of faith, hope, and love, to gain strength from him and abide by the words he taught with the gospels. God's son touched the earth to bear our sins and die. He overcame the sting of death with his resurrection, which awaits all mankind. Let the Lord be a lasting example for us to follow when problems in our lives become unbearable and hopeless to bear.

God heard his cries, 'Father, forgive them,' and 'Why have you forsaken me?' Pain engulfed him, and tears of blood were shed. God responded by lifting him up from suffering to eternal life in heaven.

After Christ's death, a gradual following of Christianity began to take place across the world, with people beginning to gain an understanding of the gospels and that life on earth is temporary, preparing us for an everlasting one.

End of message, thank you, Irene.

The Lamb

A vile of poison being sent, will be returned have faith and trust me.

12
Crucifixion

My path was a solitary one to do my father's will and be crucified. I looked up to the sky and called out to the father. The clouds parted for me, rain fell from heaven, and thunder roared across the sky as I was taken up to the Father. Shattering pain surged through my body from the nails that pierced my wrists and feet, from the tree of agony.

The tree had waited for me since my birth and for my blood that flowed freely down my body into the ground. This suffering gave me a deeper understanding of my faith as I drifted into a comatose condition. I was exhausted and in a state of dehydration as I was nailed to the cross and then lifted into an upright position.

My mother's tears of pain pierced my heart as she suffered every agonizing torture that I was given, leaving her with a tear-stained face of suffering. Thunder roared across the sky, and rain poured down on her as she stood by my cross. Her clothes clung to her rain-drenched figure as she stood grief-stricken beside me.

Looking down at her from where I hung, everything was blurry, and my body felt lighter. Then I passed through the clouds that opened into the sky above. Visions of my earthly life flashed before me of my mother, family life, and disciples, together with the disciple who had initiated my destiny.

Tormented cries came from the earth with sorrow. The enemy prowled closer with satisfaction about my impending death. The sting of death raged around me, with memories gradually fading into a hazy confusion of what was taking place. I wondered if I was still on earth.

Then I felt the overpowering presence of the enemy as he drew closer to me, and I drifted into an oblivious state. Visions filled my mind from the past. I found it hard to breathe, and was oblivious as I was filled with a bright white light that surrounded me, lifting me higher into the sky. My senses drifted into nothingness, with no sense of pain or time. I floated upwards in a tranquil state to my Father's house.

My experience of suffering on the cross has been written about by various people over time, sometimes with a lack of understanding that it was my destiny to do this for mankind. The gospels were to be spread around the world after my life on earth ended. It's a rare experience being part of God's Holy Spirit, one that very few people can attain or understand. I was destined to touch your life as you were mine through the Spirit during this time on earth, which can implant a deeper understanding of faith and spirit and what can be achieved.

Ask people to pray, pray, pray in Jesus's name, who remains close to everyone who is suffering. Also, I advise everyone to have periods of silence during your day to allow faith and peace to enter. Trust God's messages that Irene interprets on my behalf, as she has become a channel for me to use to do God's work on earth.

God bless her

My time with her is a great pleasure for me, thank you again for interpreting the messages.

13
Celebrate Easter

This message is to wish everyone around the world a peaceful and joyful Easter. From the King of the Jews who hung on the cross to gain power on earth for God's kingdom, when the sky opened and He ascended to the Father, let the joy of His resurrection reach out to people everywhere. May it heal your sufferings and ease your mental or physical pains. Peace be with you all and with Irene.

Having faith in me will help heal your bodies from illness and take away various afflictions from those still living in darkness. Allow the dawn of Easter to bring hope into your lives, sent with God's unfailing love. Let healing penetrate your bodies and souls in Jesus's name, with the joyful tidings of Easter.

The Lamb's blood was shed for the atonement of sins. Sing praises to the King of Peace and glorify the Lord forever, the Redeemer of sinners, and Creator of all creatures who inhabit the earth, sea, and sky. Continue writing, Irene, and follow the father's wishes.

The Lord chooses people who have gifts such as yours as messengers to help spread the word. Life on earth lasts for a brief period; the eternal one is a goal to aim for. Many people remain like lost sheep for far too long, and by reading and studying my messages, you can return to the right path for your lives.

Having faith can change your lives if you follow the light. The world you live in can easily introduce you to darkness. Let me guide you to find peace, breaking the chains that hold you in mental and physical bondage.

Pray for the sick and for changes to take place in the lives of the poor and in your own. I lived and experienced life on earth and died for sins to be forgiven, rising from the sting of death. Likewise, you can too, my brothers and sisters around the world. Life consists of a beginning and an end, a gift from God.

Let Easter bring a new understanding of why Irene is writing these messages for this book to be published when completed. It is to bring people on earth a greater understanding of one's life. God rules over everyone's destiny to a certain degree. Irene's was to gain knowledge and find her holy grail of peace. Trust me, brothers and sisters across the world, you can all be set free from whatever is stopping you from achieving your goals in life. Be faithful to God, and you'll find what you're searching for.

Miracles do take place with abundant light, and various people see visions, which are gifts from the Lord. Irene's experience is a good example of a quest she has been on for many years, which she should tell others about to give them hope with their worst dilemmas. This quest transformed her life. God knows the answer to her issues, not the churches she has visited. Why she was chosen out of millions of people is a secret only God can answer.

I am the light in the darkness. Without light, there is despair, depression, and thoughts of hopelessness, which bring ongoing physical and mental disorders into your bodies and lives. May healing reach whoever is reading my words, and may my peace be with you.

14
Understanding Life

To understand life, look at it simply through a child's eyes if you've temporarily lost your way. This perspective can help you find the path back and identify who you are. Everything in life can be recovered if you gain confidence in your relationship with God, whose guidance can help you break the chains of bondage in your life. This freedom allows you to move on with your life.

Being with Irene has shown me a variety of things I never experienced in my lifetime on earth. Although my time was not lengthy, it was my destiny to fulfil. Let me help you understand life better if you seek freedom from an existence, you feel trapped in, so you can achieve your victory.

Praying and meditation help still the mind and can be beneficial for recovering from various mental and physical illnesses. If the enemy controls your health issues through vices, stand firm on the rock that is there for you all. Be patient with your long-term sufferings; though they might plague your body and mind, they can be healed over time.

During my lifetime on earth, I cast out unclean spirits from people suffering from illnesses caused by strongholds of spirits. These spirits, which exist in the world, attach themselves to people's bodies and lives. They aim to take up residence in a person's body and life, controlling them through fear, torment, and various methods that create illness over time. This is a horrific ordeal, often written about in the Bible, which Jesus alleviated. This unseen ailment is hard for others to believe, yet many people suffer from it mentally and physically across the world, all searching for an answer to be set free. Many are innocent of what's happening to them. Christians, like Irene, a faithful believer in God, are prime targets.

Trust me, various seeds are being sown daily in people's bodies and lives, often through vices that develop deep roots, difficult to remove. These poisonous roots must be taken out, along with the weeds that have gathered over time, for the earth to be ready to bear new fruit. This new fruit is planted with positive thoughts, enabling changes to take place. Let's call it the season of plenty for new things to develop and change your lives.

This message contains some parable teachings; I hope it's understood.

15
God's Garden

Jesus came into the world to bring love, mercy, and hope into our lives. There has always been a lust for excessive power and worldly possessions, which can lead to a lack of faith in worshiping God, who created the world. People today spend their lives seeking ways to become wealthy, which isn't wrong unless it leads to corrupt lives driven by greed.

People have forgotten how to praise God, who watches over everything that takes place on the planet. He understands the trials and temptations humans confront daily, often instigated by the enemy, to lead lives with fewer worries and regulations.

Disasters happen when people neglect their responsibilities to others in their lives, such as their spouses and family members. This neglect transforms a regulated life into one of chaos. Associating with the wrong people or adopting bad habits gradually creates disastrous effects on one's life and existence.

Suddenly, the changes you've made in your life don't seem to be going as planned. Crisis begins to take hold of your new way of life, and you need help. You call out to God in an emergency, and He is surprised to hear you praying for help, as you haven't prayed or given thanks to Him for years. Many people pray daily and are accustomed to asking God for guidance or help, while others only pray when trouble strikes their lives.

My people, you must learn like a child taking its first steps until it can walk safely on its own. As an adult, you also need help from God at times to keep your feet firmly on the ground for support in dealing with the trials that can enter your lives daily. When temptations come offering what seems to be an easier life, be vigilant, as the enemy can appear in various disguises.

God created beautiful flowers and plants for His garden of life, to blossom throughout their lifetime on earth. These plants from this garden will be under constant pressure throughout their growth on earth, as they are special to God. Various storms might attempt to destroy their roots, as these plants need special soil to grow. (Well done, you are learning my ways.)

Attempts will be made through changing weather for these plants to be uprooted, wither, and die, never to bloom again. God's plan is already written for each individual on earth from birth to departure. Plants do die but can be reborn in springtime, as all living creation can.

The gardener of life ensures His plants and people are well-grounded, with their roots placed in the soil and handled with careful healing. They bloom again with healthy roots on planet earth, this time with roots planted deeper in life's soil, making them unmovable. They return to life in springtime when the darkness of winter has departed.

Each springtime, plants are reborn on earth and become fruitful once more in God's Garden. The Master gardener searches for any missing plants in the garden before planting new seeds in the ground. Some plants wither and die, while others remain beautiful for their lifetime in the garden. Only He knows why some humans outlive others in the garden of life.

When the span of life comes to an end, some people have not yet fulfilled their potential and continue on for more years. This parable explains God's creations on the earth, which unfold in a similar manner among plants, animals, birds, and the human race, made in His image.

End of message.

16
Parable Teaching

Humans were created to live and develop life on earth. Each person is as different as each grain of sand on the beach. God endures in the hearts of men and women, with our faith sustaining us in good and difficult times. So, we call on Him to answer our prayers, often experiencing a waiting period before a prayer is answered. Usually, the solution comes when we least expect it. Have faith that prayers are heard and answered.

God is merciful to people; He is a friend and teacher, and a loving shepherd of His flock. He lived on earth as we do, suffered death, and through His resurrection guides us as Christians. This means we might have to bear certain hardships during our lifetime and carry our own crosses. Throughout the ages, the enemy has continued attacking Christians and putting the blame on God, who bears His people's sufferings and keeps them alive, helping them survive the battle with Satan and his host of fury, who still roam the earth.

Remember, all types of attacks are happening daily to God's people, who often ask, 'Why me?' The answer is simple: because you belong to God. The enemy knew this from the beginning of your ordeal in Turkey, Irene, when your trial began. You were steadfast in your belief in God, which made you feel that God was speaking to you. I'm sure this was the case. Since that conversation began, your life and body have been in jeopardy with attacks of religious abuse from strongholds. May the Sacred Heart of Jesus be with you each passing day, bringing peace, love, and joy.

Tell people about your experience of living with devils attached to your body and explain what a devastating experience this is.

Repeat what God's Son experienced with the devil's temptations in the desert that He overcame. You are not chastised, but admired for your power and endurance over evil. Very few people on earth have lived such a lengthy trial of suffering, being tormented daily in their lives.

God loves you and knows of your trials with the forces of spiritual darkness. The meaning of life, which Christ preached, was taught with parables that became the gospel teachings to help people with their lives. Reach out, take Jesus' hand, and He'll teach you, His ways; by doing this, you'll gradually find your Holy Grail of Peace.

17
Temptations

Seek not the peace of the world, but eternal peace which is everlasting. This type of peace comes to a person when they understand God's will and are given grace from the Lord. Finding peace lies within these messages and is a universal gift that everyone can attain and use in their life. This could bring universal peace to a world full of strife and turmoil, keeping us further away from the enemy's snares that are ready and waiting to tempt us each day.

If you're reading this message and already trapped by any temptation of the enemy or complying with ways that are contrary to God's, your body is in danger as a victim and will become filled with sins of the flesh, which can lead to an early death.

I repeat, beware of the devil who can come in various disguises, and it might be in the form of a new friend who's already converted to the path of destruction, encouraging you to join them and leave the life you have behind. With invitations like, "Why don't you learn to enjoy yourself instead of living a humdrum existence?"

When someone suggests this to you, it might be a web of deception and a route to disaster, or it could be for your own good. You must decide. For any individual to stop living their usual daily life they exist by, before changing your lifestyle, you might start to be attacked by various spirits who attach themselves to a person's body. Over time, the person who's living a new lifestyle can slowly become ridden with illness and pain, along with suicidal thoughts and depression.

Although we think God is not with us, He is steadfast for His people who are suffering. But in turn, everyone must repent of their sins and renounce the enemy to be set free. As the serpent is always poised, waiting to strike God's people, it must be stopped from taking what belongs to the Father, who will never surrender Christians to the enemy or abandon them. Prayers are a powerful force that allows love to emerge with every hour they're prayed, taking a person further away from the chains of bondage and oppression, gradually setting a person free in Jesus' name.

Here ends the message.

18
Alpha and Omega of Life

This message is for people of all ages, to let you know that my love endures forever. I'm with you and will never desert anyone. May my peace be with you. Have faith in your Savior, who believes each individual person matters, whoever you are, and who is waiting to lighten your burdens. Divine love is from God, who never fails to help people in distress. Also, for those on the path of enlightenment with their faith, to gain knowledge that will help you travel safely through your life.

Irene, if you visit churches with the messages and they're rejected, or your books and talks, walk away. Don't put pressure on anyone or yourself. The messages must be read and taught freely in churches that accept the messages and open their doors. Jesus will enter those doors, and the churches will be blessed. Those who reject me are not following my way of Christianity but make their own laws using my name to gather people. If I'm rejected, I understand. Walk away from those places; don't fret or worry.

Healing is being sent daily to people who are suffering and to you. Have faith, it's the truth. Understand that the forces of darkness are still at war with God and use people like yourself as scapegoats for religion. My people, allow the Lord to guide your footsteps to finding peace. Be mindful of my words. Every one of you, find time to rest and don't fret; it causes ill health. May peace and hope of a new life for you begin with my words. For my people around the world who might have experienced or been touched by the realms of darkness, you can be healed and become whole again.

19
Powers of Contact

Respect your parents and be faithful to God by praying, reading, and understanding the Gospels, and love thy neighbour. Pray for the second coming of faith in the world that gains a worthy flock for the Father through my words. Let churches preach my messages with a human touch so people accept Jesus as a friend.

I've been close to many people on earth at various times but failed to recognize it was happening with my connection. So, no seeds were planted or grew, but faded like dead leaves in autumn. Let men and women hear my words, Irene, so my messages can bear lasting fruit. To use during their lifetime and to pass on to their children, that can grow into strong family trees that can develop into a forest that spreads across the world for the Father.

Bless you, my child, for being a channel of hope for me. As very few people have the power of contact to write the messages for me, it's a rare gift to find in the world. After experiencing such trials in your life, and by writing down my words, you'll gradually be set free. Please give my messages to your group, to other Christians, and to those without faith.

When the Gospels are read in churches, their meanings are often not understood, or how they were taught with parables. We need to pray for peace in the world and for wars to end, which can only be done by countries negotiating together to end the suffering wars bring to the human race.

Also, teach people about the enemy's tactics, as many Christians think he doesn't exist, which might help keep them away from the destructive path he offers many people to take.

You've experienced the enemy's ways, so you can explain through my words and show people the difference between God and Lucifer. As you are one of the rare people who understand what I tell you with our connection, which enables us to work together for the good of the human race.

Let light enter your lives each day, and my words become a book of value. The Bible has been altered various times since it was first written by different people over the centuries and is not exactly how events took place during my lifetime on earth. Very few people actually knew me well and how I preached the Gospels, which was done to gain people for the Father, with the development of Christianity as a religion, which continued on after my crucifixion.

Irene, thank you again for continuing to write the messages.

20
God Rules

No weapon forged against you will prevail, and you will refute every tongue that accuses you. This is the heritage of the servants of the Lord, and this is their vindication from me. Isaiah 54:17

Draw near and listen to words of wisdom, and learn that you are all God's children. Look to the heavens and see visions of the army of saints and prophets, who walked with God's grace, following the path that was laid down for them.

God's infinite power makes the dawn rise and the sun set, the oceans flow at His command, and the rain falls to wash the earth clean. The desert heats and cools at His command. The Lord rules over everything from the Alpha to the Omega, and to the end of time. Place your trust in Him, who can lead you to the truth and to the divine path of universal life from the Father.

As a messenger, you can preach the truth of good and evil as you've experienced both, which have existed in the world since time began on earth. Let Solomon's wisdom guide you, and David be a shining example, and me your light in the darkness. You are worthy to receive my words, Irene, and chosen for this work as part of your life.

Let people follow in the Lord's footsteps and believe in Him, who was born to be exalted and to wear purple and white on His journey. Try wearing these colours too, my people, in finding your holy grails of peace. The seeds of sorrow can be sown and grow, which can create havoc for any of God's people.

By writing the messages, you are doing God's work and chosen for this task. All of your prayers are heard and will be answered by God. Believe in God's power in the world, and that people like Irene can be contacted through the Holy Spirit. Also, know that I am close to you all when you pray. Peace be with you.

21
Visions of Life

Do the stars ever cease to shine or the sun lose its powerful rays of light, which it sends to the earth for creation to grow each passing year? Does rain stop falling from above, helping the earth evolve? All these wondrous things come from God's mighty hand, while the human race continues to destroy many of them.

When a wounded bird falls from the sky, it can learn to fly again once its damaged wing heals. Then it's able to soar high in the sky and fly away. If a sparrow can survive the trials of life, so can we.

Life consists of many changes as the years go by, which we bear and endure as humans, adjusting to hardships when they take place in our lives. When illness or the death of a loved one strikes to ruin our life, catastrophes happen every day to good people, and during those periods, God silently continues clearing disasters from people's lives.

How does God demonstrate that He's alive in the world? I believe it's done by choosing people carefully whom He can use as messengers or in other ways to communicate through the Holy Spirit to the world. The Lord remains watching over us, like a father caring for his children. You've achieved a great deal, Irene, by surviving up to the present day, living with what you've experienced, and remaining faithful to God.

The world is rapidly changing, and a majority of people are turning towards what's offered through the media for fame and fortune. They seem to have forgotten God's teachings and their meanings. Let's hope the messages bring some changes in the society you live in for the better, through my words, for people to know that the Lord still exists.

The human race is God's creation, and He watches carefully, noticing all the changes that take place in the world. Be vigilant and pray for a better world with God's guidance, so fewer people choose the enemy's path of destruction. Churches must keep the word strong and alive, with the same contents of the tablet, for people to return to worship God by their own free will.

When mankind breaks the laws that God approved, the enemy has easy access to enter and corrupt people's lives, inciting them into becoming victims of various vices, which ruin their lives. Every person has a path to follow from birth, and you might stray from it. If this is the case, search to find the way back with God's help. Life is a gift from God, and many families are waiting to be parents blessed with children.

Beware of unrighteous people offering gifts of no value, which can bring disaster to anyone obsessed with the idea of being rich. Wealth isn't bad if used wisely and not wasted solely on oneself, without a thought for others who are less fortunate in life. Owning large amounts of possessions can be a delight for some people and a burden for others if it teaches a person nothing worthwhile, only the satisfaction of being rich. A balanced life will find contentment, which is a passing phase of life we experience that doesn't last.

End of message.

22
Parables Transformed to Gospels

God is the head of the church, not for those who deceive the law by preaching the word without applying it by example. Let mercy, faith, and love guide your path as an example for others to follow who are true followers of Christ.

Listen to the gospel readings in church, and understand that some of the stories vary from the way Jesus originally preached them. Keep an open mind when discussing the gospels to find the truth within each one, from what you've learned by hearing them. Jesus likes the gospels to be discussed and taught to his disciples using parables as teaching methods.

Over time, stories from the gospels have been changed as they were passed down by word of mouth and rewritten throughout the years. Many of the original teachings are slightly different from how they were originally told. This can easily happen when words are passed down by word of mouth and then written by various people after the death of Jesus.

I ask people to be unmovable like a rock and stand firm when dealing with the trials of life, and to be strong in faith. Also, consider me equal to a father and friend in your life. Irene listens and trusts me, so you can tell people I'm here to help you all. Many people around the world are suffering from long-term illnesses and are crying out for help, as you have to me.

God finds suitable ways to send healing for each person's individual needs. Help is always being sent to you, even though you may doubt it, through a loving, caring soul who is helping you, as well as many other people who have health issues. During my time on earth, I was weary too, like many of you are, and my father held me up in those times so I could continue my work and teach the word to the people on earth in that period. The gospels were needed then as they are today, for people to live better lives and gain insight into finding peace within oneself and with others. People must learn to respect and believe in God, whatever religion they follow.

Christianity began with my birth on earth, and my mission was to teach and preach the word of God to the people, for them to grow in the light from a small seed into a fruitful vine, which could continue to grow throughout their life and be carried on by future generations.

End of message.

23
Shores of Knowledge

The sea lies dormant until the next wave washes onto the beach, carrying the sand away to different shores with the tide. Let your life be carried to new shores of the knowledge of God's truth and understanding. These messages are for people to renew their faith in Him, who hung on the tree to gain freedom for us.

I am the light, so let me shine in the darkness into your lives. God sent His Son into the world for people to be redeemed back to Him and for people to know that God remains vigilant, keeping watch over the world and its people. This means people can be absolved from their sins and return to the flock, from the darkness or despair they might be experiencing in their lives.

Tell little children to come unto me; I'll be their light in the darkness. If they're suffering with fear from abusive parents, who should be their rock to develop upon throughout their life, let them find comfort. Many adults are also living with unresolved abusive relationships. Life can be a tedious and a hard journey to bear, depending on the path you travel, with many trials of suffering.

Let children help their parents over the passing years, so parents know they have someone to rely on for help when needed on their life's journey. Parents' needs increase over the years, and children should be there for them. Respect, love, and honour what God has given you as parents and family on earth. Brothers and sisters, be close to each other and never disrespect your father or mother. They're a gift from God to guide you from your birth.

A well-adjusted family can teach a child what family life consists of, which prepares a child for a stable life as they gradually transform into an adult. This can be a blessing for any child to have their family roots planted firmly in the ground by the grace of God.

So, plant your seeds deep, and they'll flourish in the soil, then develop over time into a mountain of good things that are gifts from above, equal to the rays of sunlight which penetrate the earth to bring forth crops of wheat, with the help of man's persistence to Plow the fields and reap the harvest.

Families can also reap rewards if their children's seeds are planted in fertile ground from a young age. There's no time like the present to start learning about the Lord's gifts of love for His people. So, let your roots develop by planting them deep, achieving a wondrous success.

End of message

My messenger is dearly loved. I will begin to show signs for you to believe it's me; no one else is doing this task.

Thank you for your patience. God bless you.

24
Seasons of Life

This message aims to bring a deeper understanding to people about how one's life evolves, as each individual is created by God. Consider your life akin to the changing of seasons. Human life unfolds similarly to the growth of a plant, starting with the planting of a seed and developing with the birth of a child. This part of a child's life is akin to springtime.

For a child to develop and grow, its roots must be firmly planted. Proper grounding by parents is essential for the child to evolve correctly over time. Every child needs guidance to set their path in the right direction. As the child develops mentally and physically, the next phase of life begins, which we can call summertime. This phase offers greater freedom as the child's body, mind, and views on life develop.

During this gradual process, parental nurturing is necessary to guide the child in the right direction. Teaching them about life will help shape their future from teenagers to adults. As they leave childhood behind, children need continuous guidance to stay on the right path.

Some children's journeys can be traumatic with their transition from teenagers to adults. Guidance at this stage must be gradual, allowing them to gain knowledge and understanding of the world. By listening and learning, they can gain wisdom each day, enabling better communication with others. Mankind can develop into an everlasting flower if well-planted, growing anywhere in the world, traveling safely through life, and arriving at a safe harbour.

As the seasons change from summer to autumn, so does human life. In autumn, people often reflect on their past mistakes and the wrong roots planted that have grown into regrets. This is a time to start uprooting those mistakes, daunting as it may be, and begin the process of forgiveness before winter sets in. Forgiving others and oneself is crucial for clearing the path before the sun sets on one's life.

This act of forgiveness brings peace and joy, allowing for a new understanding and hope for better things. It leads to greater self-acceptance and inner peace over the years. Eventually, everyone arrives at the last season of life: winter. In this season, fears about the future and the effects of aging arise. It's important to remain strong, trusting in God to help you through this part of your journey.

God understands the pains of illness and suffering. Remember, you are never alone, whether in hospitals, nursing homes, or living alone. Trust and believe that God is with you through every pain and sorrow. Never fear death, for it is only the declining of the outer body while the soul departs to a higher place in glory with the Father. God's love for His children is eternal, from birth through the final stage of life.

His mercy and devotion come from deep within His heart, accompanying you throughout your earthly journey. When life ends, it gives birth to a new life beyond the earthly body. God holds the key to the veil between the two worlds. Never fear the end of life, for those who believe in Christ Jesus have a new beginning. Have faith that God waits for all His people.

I've explained briefly to Irene my views on the decline of the human race, and she will convey them as best as she can. All living things on earth are born and die in creation. God is the creator of all life, and everything functions similarly from the seeds planted to the animal kingdom and the human race. All creatures have a lifespan to live and die, functioning similarly after materializing and deteriorating over time.

Everything on the planet has a life force similar in nature. Humans, like plants, grow and blossom. Some people have long lives, others short, depending on their conditions and circumstances. This is the similarity among all living things created and controlled by God.

Emphasize to everyone that they have a choice to believe or not what I'm asking you to write for this book. It is your choice, as an individual with a mind of your own, to believe in the creation of the world and God. The world did not create itself, nor could the vast planet we inhabit have appeared without help from someone mightier than us. I hope you do not remain stagnant in disbelief of the wonders of creation designed by God. I'm not forcing you to believe my views; you can deny my existence. But I will remain waiting with outstretched arms, like any father would for his children's return.

The Lamb

25
Realms of Darkness

My experience of trials during my lifetime on earth was for the ransom for mankind on the tree, for those who believe in my resurrection. Always be just and merciful to others, and you'll receive mercy from God, our Creator. Don't lose faith or hope; let these tools become your shield and buckler for deliverance. For those people who are waiting for an answer to end their suffering, let Jesus become your guide and friend. Don't doubt what I give you to write; the messages are coming through the Holy Spirit for this book.

God has never harmed you or any of His children throughout their lives, and He weighs up the trials they endure. Blessings to the people who continue to follow Jesus after suffering various trials that might be caused by the enemy. By reading my words, I know you're one of my children who has never rejected God. He will find a plan for your future happiness, so don't give up on whatever you might be going through at this time in your life, it will end. Healing might take a while for various people, but it is in motion and will take place for the older or younger generation who have suffered a lengthy time.

Many people are under various different types of attacks daily that could be coming from the enemies' wiles going on around the world. People who become victims have no knowledge or idea of what's going on mentally or physically in their bodies, or that it's being done by strongholds of depraved, unclean spirits of the worst type who attach themselves to people.

Once unclean spirits attach themselves, their attacks on the victim begin. With an intent to destroy the victim's life and health, these unseen attacks on the body or attached to it can't be seen, causing suffering for many people.

These types of tormenting methods are still being used today by strongholds of spirits as they were in Jesus' time on earth, where He cast them out of people in stories in the Bible. These spirits are assassins who come with the sole intent to corrupt a person's body and mind, leading to insanity or suicidal tendencies after continuous attacks. This will never take place if you continue praying to God. I'll be with you.

People grow frailer through these attacks, and that's when the enemy will attack a victim more, filling their body with infirmities and suffering. May peace come to all my people who are suffering when least expected. Jesus would never harm any person and healed many people during His lifetime on earth.

This is the enemy's campaign to ruin your existence. Loyalty, goodness, family life, love, and friendship are not on the enemy's agenda. Destruction is the number one rule for him and his followers, aiming to ruin souls with perversion, corruption, and vices of every kind.

Pray to Our Lady for her help, for your children to find the right person to spend their life with, and to bless your families and homes. Let God's light become a part of your lives, and His messages help you all, my people. Let prayer and praise to God become a daily function like breathing, which will keep you all alive.

Blessings to the person reading these words at this moment in time.

26
God Doesn't Want Suffering

No one is ordered to suffer by God. Instead, if you've sinned, you are called to repentance, and He will give mercy and strength to His people. Have faith that God sends help to relieve infirmity, pain, and suffering. Sickness can stem from various fears we live with daily. So, my people, be happier, and by doing so, you allow healing to take place in your bodies and minds more quickly.

Also, learn to believe in the power of the Lord, and it will come to pass. The spirit of goodness is endearing, but many times it is seen as weakness by those you encounter daily. As Christians, you are my children, and want you all to understand that you are never alone, I am always with you, so trust me.

My crucifixion and suffering were my joy because they ensured that you are all on the path of salvation in a truly wonderful way, a path I once walked on Earth a long time ago. Be merciful in how you treat others, and mercy will be given unto you. I take no pleasure in any Christian suffering; I want you to know this is the truth. Each person has a calling to achieve in their life, sent by the father, and each man or woman must do what feels right for them. So, avoid the enemy's wiles that aim to change the course you have chosen for your life if unclean spirits appear to disrupt it.

The world is diverse today, with many people living dangerously with various freedoms and lifestyles, which open doors for realms of spiritual darkness to enter. The younger generation is unaware that their bodies can be easily trapped in a world of spiritual darkness. When this happens, people develop a hatred for God as they become victims of various evil spirits by mixing with the wrong people, not realizing their lives are heading for disaster.

The world of corruption leads any victim down a path to their own destruction over time, with various crimes, vices, and deeds committed against God's laws. The rulers of darkness are generally in charge when this happens, with demonic spirits whose goal is to destroy people's lives. The signs are evident, but no one seems to notice what's going on when a person's character changes. They listen to gossip, believe lies, and enjoy watching violent and oppressive acts of sadistic cruelty on TV and in films.

People can be attacked from a supernatural plane daily and have no idea this is happening, as it is unseen. You have no idea you are being mentally attacked on a supernatural plane as your interest grows in horror movies. Violent and frightening horror scenes in films can have a devastating mental effect, which we never realize. Spiritual forces of wickedness could be at work through various circumstances in our lives. You're not sleeping well, and your working life becomes hard to bear because you're tired but still up late watching horror films.

I don't want to overload whoever is reading this book with my personal views, but we all need basic faith to keep us on course in our vessel of life. God is the light of the world and says, 'No demon or stronghold can take what belongs to the Father and destroy it if the child is not willing.' I am the light of the world who will bring lasting peace to end all of your nightmares. Irene, your name translates in Greek as peace, may it be with you.'

Jesus knew the enemy and what he offered brought destruction and chaos to the world, with corruption and roots of wickedness for human minds and bodies. Some people will follow what he offers, leading to a despairing existence of utter misery, death, and suicide if you accept the father of lies and the games he plays with human lives.

Keep the Holy Family in your life, along with the angels and saints. Roses have thorns, so treasure the graces you have been given and enjoy the world around you, my people. Our Lady was steadfast in her ways, and Jesus showed mercy to those with infirmities. Speak, and He listens to all who pray with faith to Him. The cross is a symbol of life and a sign of new beginnings to bring health and peace back into your lives in many ways. My angels and saints are standing guard, praying for everyone to be restored to health, happiness, and my peace. Bless you, daughter.

The Lamb.

God is real, and with each day, your friendship group will begin to experience greater peace in your lives.

27
Stand Firmly on the Rock

The path of each person is laid before a child takes its first breath of life into the world, with God watching over each person for most of their journey on earth. He is there to guide and help when a person strays from their path and loses their way, possibly through the temptations offered to everyone daily in the world. Various sins one might indulge in can cause them to turn away from God.

As the shepherd of my flock, I search for any missing sheep that are lost until they are found and returned to their rightful path and to the Master of the flock. In many cases, the lost sheep refuses to follow the path back that's being shown to return safely to the shepherd.

As the father of my flock, I remain waiting patiently at the crossroads of life for the lost sheep's return. This could take a lifetime of waiting until the lost sheep returns to the flock. Jesus's patience is everlasting, as is His mercy for His children deeper and wider than any ocean that flows on through time and eternity with the love He holds for His people.

This short message is to let people know that I understand the number of temptations a person faces during their lives on earth, which makes the path we are given easy to stray from. Through the number of temptations, we face during a lifetime on earth, keep your feet placed firmly on the Rock I can build for you to stand upon, which is immovable. It's the only gift that can direct you back onto the right path for your life.

Stand firm like a rock that nothing can destroy.

End of message.

28
Seashore of life

The seashore lies dormant until the next wave breaks against it, carrying the sands of time back into the sea. Until the sand reaches distant shores with the incoming tides of life. Let your life be carried to new shores of knowledge with God's ways and words, with the messages given for people to renew their faith and belief in Jesus, who hung on the tree and drank the cup as a ransom to free you.

Gain hope in being redeemed by Jesus through the truth, as He is the light of the world and can turn darkness into light, which is needed in the world today. Aim to be peaceful, don't fret. Repeat these words to people you meet who want to be freed from ailments and suffering. Be still in the sacred heart of Jesus and be healed with His love. Let Him be your guiding light in the changing patterns of life in the world, teaching you His ways and guiding your footsteps the right way for your journey through life.

Be your parents' hope throughout the passing years with all they need. Time passes quickly, and their needs increase, so always be there for them to give them a helping hand during their life's journey. Respect, love, and honour what God has given you as your family on earth. Be close to your brothers and sisters and never disrespect your parents. God sent you parents to be your guiding light from your birth, a base for you to grow from, having a good family life given by God's grace.

Plant your vines to grow and prosper on the earth with firm roots planted deeply into the soil. If the ground is fertile, this will bring forth a good crop of grain as the years pass to feed you, with the sun's rays of light that help your crops to grow. So, you can reap what we sow, may it be plentiful. God's goodness is endless towards mankind. If only we could soar high up into the sky like birds and see the wonders God has created in the world all around us. Let's stop for a moment in time and recognize God's creations.

Let love be a gateway to leading a better life. The next step is letting go of grudges with people who've hurt you. Be a child again, enjoy what you see around you as if you're seeing it for the first time. Do you ever stop for a few minutes and gaze at the beauty of the natural environment around you? Do you see the glorious colours in the changing of the seasons each year? Or notice the calm and turbulence of the seashore when there's a storm approaching, it changes within seconds.

Beginning a new stage in anyone's life takes time and can be done at any age. If a bird can fly again after having a broken wing, anyone can rebuild their broken life with faith and persistence. God cares for His people, and whatever you might be suffering with will eventually come to an end. Believe this, and it will come to pass. Let your body and mind work together in harmony for improvements with any health conditions you might be suffering, my people.

End of message

29
The Universe

Do the stars cease to shine, or does the sun lose its powerful rays of sunlight that help creation to flourish each passing year on Earth? Does the rain stop falling from the sky to the Earth so that creation can evolve? These wondrous things come from the Lord's mighty hand, which the human race continues to destroy with chemicals and gases from modern devices.

During one's journey on Earth, you see many changes taking place as the years pass by, which you face and experience in your daily lives. When a loved one is struck with ongoing trials of illness, it appears like a flash of lightning into many people's lives. This happens to all of us at some time. Catastrophes occur in many good people's lives daily. And God has the power to intervene and clear many situations that seem impossible, to bring peace and harmony back into people's lives.

Healing is also given to many people who are suffering from long-term illness and family issues. Then an answer comes from out of nowhere, resolving an ongoing problem. Has this happened to you? If it has, God might be helping you to sort things out. People never think or realize that it could be through God's mighty hand at work in the world.

God is careful with his choice of whom he wants to interpret messages through the Holy Spirit. Messengers are a channel for God to communicate with Christian people around the world. Irene has the gift from God to hear and interpret through the Holy Spirit what I tell her. Although she finds the whole experience hard to adjust to, she has been under attack for over fifty years by strongholds of unclean spirits because she possesses this gift with God's connection. The churches she visited didn't remove the demonization she was suffering from, which gradually deteriorated her health over the years. This affected her ability to do my work on Earth when she began to write her first book for God.

Consider me equal to a father who watches attentively over my people who are physically or mentally sick, along with others who are praying for peace in the world. This can only be achieved by countries learning to listen to each other and talking over their differences to bring peace around the world. I have confidence in what Irene interprets for me with this book, that it will achieve success for the Father. We have worked together throughout the years, facing many obstacles to stop my words from being written.

The world is becoming a dark place to live in, full of crimes, vices, and corruption. People are being offered large sums of money to break rules that were made for their own good, and they reap rewards for doing this. Too many people accept living a wayward existence, not realizing what the outcome will be until it's too late.

When the human race breaks the laws inscribed on the tablets, the enemy has easy access to enter people's lives with habitual sins, which may appear harmless at the time but can become lethal to destroy a person and their life.

Beware of unrighteous people bearing gifts of no value, who can incite disaster for an individual who craves wealth and prestige. Longing for large amounts of money or possessions in your life isn't bad if the wealth is used wisely and not selfishly on oneself, without a thought for other people who have very little in life. Remember, you can't take your wealth and possessions with you when your journey comes to an end on Earth. So, if you are blessed with wealth, use it wisely with a thought for others who aren't.

30
Your Never Solitary

Your never alone, as the Father knows each individual child to whom he gave the gift of life. So, if you stray onto the wrong path during your life, all you need to do is repent. You can be saved by God's grace and power, which he gives to all of his people, whom he wants with him forever, and not taken away by the enemy's false promises that can lead you to a life of sin, sorrow, and suffering beyond your imagination.

Satan tempts people to fall into his snare. You're one of mine, Irene, but many are lustful and easily caught in the trap laid for them. If they refuse to see the truth when it's shown to them, it leaves God with no power to help the ensnared victim. The human race must learn and abide by God's wisdom and knowledge written in the laws on the tablets. This helps people remain safe and free during their life and prevents them from being caught in the traps laid by the enemy for God's people.

The path we travel during our lifetime can be a weary one if we don't strive to live in harmony with each other. This can only be achieved by seeking peace with other nations and stopping fights over petty things for more power. Learning to be forgiving builds bridges and joins countries and people together across the world. Stop fighting and hurting each other by withholding forgiveness for the unjust mistakes we all make during our lifetimes on earth.

Start by doing deeds of kindness to help others on your journey through life, and never be envious of other people's wealth or position. Start your day with a different pattern of thought to find the truth for yourself of who you are, and begin to work with God's manner of teaching for changes to take place. This will bring gradual peace to you and others. I'm explaining these simple methods through my words and messages can help people start understanding and appreciating the simple things that can change and bring joy, hope, and love back into your life with everlasting peace.

The world you live in is ravaged with hatred and craving for power, creating a great deal of destruction. It must revert back to God's ways and teachings, which were written to follow.

Irene, peace be with you, my friend, and the only one who can give you lasting peace. The world is full of people living perverted, sinful lives through greed, wealth, and power, seeking contentment and happiness, who are willing to do anything to achieve these goals.

Thank you for being patient in writing what I want to say.

31
The Christ Child

At Christmas, the Christ child enters the world again each year and is born anew in a manger. His parents weren't rich in material wealth, but they were given a great treasure by God in the form of a child whose birth changed the course of history. The child was born to do God's work on earth. Jesus followed the path he was given and conquered death on the cross. That's not a journey for the faint-hearted to achieve. But let's follow the word of God, by doing things that are pleasing to him and being faithful to the word.

May His birth kindle a flame in your hearts that never dies, as the bells ring out their jubilant chimes with this Christmas message. Be joyful at this time of year when I'm reborn once more, and may my blessings, peace, and happiness be with all my people around the world.

Being born human like you were, I had the same emotions with my cries of hunger and pain like anyone else. My mother's joy at my birth was like all mothers' when she held me for the first time and gazed lovingly at me once I took my first breath of life. She was there for me over the years until I took my last breath, hung dying on the tree, when swords pierced both hearts.

Let this Christmas be a good year for everyone, with health, happiness, and well-being to sustain each person. Also, learn to be forgiving towards the people who've hurt you at this time of year. Open your heart to God, and he can bring wonderful new things into your life. Blessings and peace to you all at Christians across the world.

Let peace become abundant, with health for the sick, food for the poor, and let lonely older people know that God loves them. Tell them this, Irene, and remember that none of my people are abandoned. I am with you all until the end of time.

These words are precious and given to very few people to write, Irene, chosen through being a soldier of Christianity who has continued on relentlessly and been firm like a rock. Many people preach the gospels, but very few are chosen to work with the Holy Spirit for the Father with messages.

The Shepherd

I send peace, happiness, and blessings to the members of your prayer and friendship group.

32
Christmas Message

My message to the world is one of peace, especially as Christmas time enters our lives once more. My birth on earth at this time of year was through the Father, to renew your faith and bring Jesus into your hearts again. To live among my people once more and teach you my ways through Irene, who is interpreting my messages for this book through the Spirit.

My birth was a sign from God to bring love, joy, and hope in the form of a child. Sent from the Father to live on earth and share the word of God with the people. I grew up in a family like everyone else at that time, in an occupied country with many rules and regulations, which is now called the Holy Land. My family wasn't wealthy, but we lived a contented, normal existence, like many families of that time.

My birth into the world was predicted in the line of David, and it was foretold that I would be different, sent by God to establish Christianity through my teachings. After my death, these teachings became the Gospels through the help of my disciples.

This came to pass with the birth of Christianity, as the Gospels were taught and spread throughout the world over the years. My sacrifice and suffering on the cross brought my resurrection, overcoming the sting of death to show there is an afterlife. Having the Father's great love and support was essential during my time on earth.

Through this, I learned to understand the daily struggles people faced during that period under Roman jurisdiction. My resurrection changed the world's vision of Christianity, which continued to grow over the centuries. From a young age, I understood that being born on earth was the Father's will, which would bring forth my ministry and teachings. Later, through God's power, I healed the sick and cast out unclean spirits to set people free. Many healings took place as I travelled, teaching the word of God and ministering to the sick and suffering wherever I went.

At that time, there were few remedies for the diseases I treated. The healings occurred through the power of God's intervention. As I travelled and taught, people's interest grew in the way I taught with parables. Word of the healings spread by mouth, bringing my first Christian followers on my mission for the Father.

The teachings are simple to understand and can give a person a deeper insight into how to live their life. I hope the messages bring you a new understanding of life that you might find useful, and serve as a guide for your children, pointing them in the right direction for their lives. These messages can make a difference in one's life.

Take a chance, and read some of them.

33
Are Prayers Heard?

Are our prayers heard when we pray to the Lord and cry out to Him in despair? Do our prayers keep us safe and heal us from the suffering and trials of life?

All Christians have periods in their lives when they feel they are losing faith in praying, feeling their prayers aren't being heard or answered. Many suffer daily with health problems that have a deteriorating effect on their lives. There's a famous quotation that says, "Time is a great healer of body and soul." Can God release a person from any type of ordeal they suffer with? People say if you believe and have faith, a solution will come.

But a great number of people do have faith in God, yet find no solutions for their endless health problems. So, where does the answer lie, as many believers continue to suffer? Many are waiting at a crossroads in their lives for an answer to change their life.

For God's peace in their homes, and for family members who are sick with various types of illnesses, praying for guidance and deliverance from their long-term ailments. God understands your problems and heartaches that many of you endure during your lifetimes on earth. His mercy is endless, like an ocean flowing to people who are suffering. This includes those living in poverty with distressing conditions and diseases in various countries around the world.

Trust in Jesus' name when you pray and believe that He can help you. Also, our Lady is waiting to hear people's prayers. Churches are disciplined establishments, not trained counsellors or spiritual advisors, who have time to study the problems of each person.

"It's hard to understand God's ways," is another quote, along with "Knock and He'll answer." Understandably, most people in the world are praying for an answer for something they need or want. The world is a phenomenal size, so are we in a queue throughout our lives waiting for an answer? Life is a mystery, like God, and we are always searching to see everything that exists.

I can confirm there is another world, as I've lived in both. There is a world of darkness, mentioned in biblical terms, and the light of God, which has kept the universe revolving throughout the centuries since the beginning of time. Amen, may it continue.

Start taking your issues to God and see if you get the results you want by praying to Him. To improve your situation, you're suffering with, go to church as often as you can. By passing through that door, changes could gradually take place.

Let God be your shield and protection

34
Key to Illness

God doesn't order people to suffer, only to repent if they've sinned. He offers mercy and strength to His people. Have faith in God to help take away infirmity and suffering. Sickness is often created by oneself through the various fears or stress you live with each day. Allow yourself to be happier; by doing this, you allow healing to take place in the body and mind more quickly.

It's important to believe in the power of the Lord, as healing can be done through prayer. The spirit of goodness is endearing in a person, but often seen as weakness by other people you come into contact with daily, who have no faith in God. I consider Christian people my children, whatever age you might be. You're never alone with whatever trial you might be facing in your life at the present time. I'm always around and with you.

Crucifixion and suffering were my joy, knowing that you're all on the path of salvation in a wonderful way, taken by myself a long time ago on earth. Be merciful in the way you treat other people, and mercy will be given unto you. I don't gain pleasure from any Christian suffering; that's the truth I want you to know. Each person has a calling in their life to achieve and the freedom of choice in choosing what's right for them.

The world is a diverse place today where people are living dangerously with various freedoms and lifestyles, which can open doors for realms of spiritual darkness to enter. The younger generation seems unaware that their bodies and minds can be easily trapped in the wrong kind of world, which can develop a hatred towards God and a disciplined life. After becoming victims of various evil influences through mixing with the wrong people, some young people never realize their lives are heading for disaster.

Leading corrupt lifestyles can eventually lead to a person's own destruction over a period of time through various crimes, vices, and deeds instigated against God's laws. The enemy might be in charge of the outcome of these types of situations that happen to destroy a person's life. The signs are evident, but no one seems to notice what's actually happening when they're on the path of destruction. When this situation takes place in people's lives, changes begin to occur in their character.

They start watching violent oppressive acts of sadistic cruelty on TV and in films. People can be attacked this way from the realms of darkness, which is supernatural and unseen. Young people have no idea of what's going on; it's invisible, and they continue watching these types of films on TV. Violent, frightening horror scenes in films can have a devastating effect on us mentally, which we don't realize. Next, you're not sleeping well, and your working life becomes hard to endure as you're tired but still staying up late to watch horror films.

I don't want to bore whoever's reading this message, that's my personal view, as we all need to have a basic faith in our lives to keep us on the right track. God is the light of the world, and no manifestations or realms of darkness can take away what belongs to the Father if the person is not willing to follow and be destroyed.

I'm the light of the world who can bring lasting peace to end your nightmares. 'Irene, are you still there? Your name translates in Greek as peace; may it be with you.'

35
Life's Journey on Earth

Your journey through life can be one of great discoveries in the world where you live for a brief period of time on earth. The one beyond the veil is eternal, and it's the goal to aim for. If you've been one of my lost sheep for a lengthy time, aim to become safer by having faith in God. Then, your life can start to take a different course gradually. Although at present it might seem pointless at times, as though your life is over, it's not. It is about to begin a new chapter, trust me.

I am the light in the darkness, so let me guide you in finding the truth and peace for your body and mind. Most issues in life can be resolved by following Jesus' guidance, which can be done through prayer and reading the Bible when you have time. By doing this, a greater meaning will begin to appear in your life.

I was a man on earth, not a monument; God's son who died for the sins of mankind so they could be forgiven, and who rose from the sting of death with my resurrection. My people, the trials you might be suffering with in your lives can have solutions. First, you must learn to still your mind, which can be achieved through meditation. This can be done by reading a parable or psalm from the Bible, or a verse with meaning for you from a book or poem.

Be still, take time to read what you choose, then contemplate its meaning. Letting go of things can be difficult and takes time but must be done. To gain control over a situation or health issue you might have, the first step is to learn how to let go of negative thoughts that appear in your mind. Gaze at nature's beauty all around you the sky above, a sunset, and the rolling incoming waves by the seashore. All things have a beginning and an end; keep this in mind.

36
My Visions

Over the years, I've had various religious visions, being a sensitive and medium, and some were incredible, like watching a moving film. I was privileged to see through the eyes of a supernatural world.

One vision that I remember clearly was of Our Lady, with various scenarios from her family life in Nazareth with a small Jesus. When the vision began, he was a small, happy child talking with his mother in their hometown of Nazareth, behaving like any small boy would. His mother was busy cleaning their house and arranging clothes that had been washed outside to dry. As the vision unfolded before me, changes began to take place, with Jesus' materializing into different ages until he was a fully grown man.

Then, he was walking a sun-drenched path, carrying the cross with its full weight bearing down on him, to his crucifixion on the hill of the skull. With the weight of the cross crushing down on him, struggling under the weight of the tree, sweat poured down his face, mixed with hues of blood from the Crown of Thorns, which pierced his head. His translucent image was covered with blood, sweat, and tears that flowed down his entire torso. I could hear Our Lady's agonizing sobs each time he fell under the weight of the cross. He rose, lifted the cross, and persevered towards the hill to die.

His mother was beside him on that everlasting journey towards the hill. The sun's penetrating rays beat down on both, with a mist rising from the heat surrounding them. Wreathed with pain, he fell once more, blood flowing from his body and soul into the ground. Enduring trials that he was born to accomplish and bear, no power on earth could separate them, not even the sting of death, which waited on the hill. Mother and son gradually became a beaming light, through love, anguish, and pain, bonding them forever in eternity. She reached out to help him bear the weight of the cross and made a wild attempt to lift one end. Jesus stretched his hand to stop her, grasping her hand in his. He fell again, taking the full weight of the cross to stop his beloved mother from lifting the tree meant for him. Crowds of people followed them to see the spectacle of his crucifixion, surging forward towards Christ and his mother, being abusive, pushing, shouting, and spitting at them.

It was unbearable grief for a mother, from deep within her soul, knowing the horrendous ordeal that lay ahead for both, which must be endured together. That was captured in time at his crucifixion, when both hearts are pierced by arrows as he dies on the cross. Both were born to bear this suffering together, with dignity, devotion, and pain, on that day on the hill of Golgotha. Tears of sorrow were left on that sun-drenched path, with heat engulfing both, together with the fiery pains of her son's battle-scarred body on the hill of Calvary.

The resurrection came after the sting of death, bringing new life with the risen Christ. Tears flowed that day like rain falling from heaven down her beautiful, tear-stained face, with grief and sorrow that reached the depths of her soul. This united them with a cloak of hope from this world into the next, where his glory was written.

Each individual is given free will from birth, so they might find one of the massages helpful. I believe these teachings have been given to me as a messenger by the Holy Spirit from God, to help people make changes in their lives on earth for the better. That could benefit and change the course of their lives, as the words of the messages hold great power and are all meaningful about life's human sufferings, including temptations we all face every day.

I hope that by sharing my gift of the word with others, Jesus, might also help the person reading my words to find your own holy grail of health and peace.

Pray as you do for the sick, hungry, and poor, and for a new life to start taking place for you, with greater meaning this time. This applies to all my children who are stationary or suffering within their lives.

Blessings and my peace to you.

37
Author's View of Good and Evil

Do you believe or not, the Lord's healing power is active and being sent to people around the world to alleviate illness, pain, and suffering? The Lord's power can erase various health problems that might be sent by the realms of darkness. There are two powers in the world: good and evil. Do you believe and honour God, then stand firm on the rock He built for you? Although very few people will ever see God, millions of people continue believing. Your faith has given you substantial evidence that he is with us, a living entity to call upon when we are in distress or at the end of our earthly life.

Many people's journey through life can be a hard and painful one, depending on where they are born and grow up. Does God know the answer to the outcome of your life? If you're a believer, you trust in the Lord, and that He will not fail to find the answer for what you need. This might take time, as Rome wasn't built in a day.

If you're reading this book, you must have faith in God or be interested in seeing what these messages are about, which I say I've been given through spirit, physically being a sensitive. The choice is yours to believe what I've written or not.

I've spent nearly fifty years puzzling over the theory of good and evil and living with the reality of the subject daily. The two are at war daily in the world that we all live in. Temptation has a strong foothold in the world today, and people are too complacent about discipline and common sense.

Many people follow Christianity without understanding what's written in the Bible, with the teachings, and their true meaning behind the words they've read, so they remain blind to the truth.

By searching, a person learns through their trials and mistakes, and by the lessons they've learned through trial and error, they reach the truth with the teachings from God. In Christ, there's light and life that only a few of the purest hearts can find with true faith.

I know you're still on your journey and that God is well pleased with you, so your conclusion is growing closer to ending your journey. But the issue attached to your body is a demon of destruction, aiming to make you commit suicide. You've waited so long for deliverance without an answer, so don't despair at having no response from God. He is with you.

Your visions that puzzle you, are from the demonic attachment and not from God. My people whatever you might be suffering with continue praying to God to be set free. Irene's experiences are an example, as she's been shown incredible visions from God. The ones that confused her came from the enemies' attachments, not trust God's visions. That explains clearly how the enemy works.

38
Life's Laws

To keep your path of life clear follow God's simple laws, which can create a mountain of benefits in your lives. If you learn to adjust to them over time, they will also help guide your children in the right direction through their lives. This can be done by following a few simple rules from the Father and being under the shadow of His wings, safe and free from harm, to protect your children throughout their life.

I remain close to my people throughout each one's life, to protect and be their shield in times of trouble. I wait with outstretched arms to catch each one if they fall on the journey of life. I will hold you up until the storms have passed and calmed. Learn to trust and believe my words, and in the manner, I'm giving them to Irene to interpret, they will give whoever reads this a great understanding of the ways I taught people about life. These are the ways we all have to face daily and deal with when life's trials strike us during our lives on earth. Every type of suffering can be frustrating to live with for many years. People might sympathize, but no one realizes the stress and pain you're going through except you, every moment of your life.

It's not of men I speak, but of Almighty God, who believes that if His children stray from the path that's laid down for them by His hand, he hopes they find a way to repent and return to God. He remains waiting for the return of each lost sheep that's strayed from its path and lost its way. As over time, weeds can grow and need tending to, and the path needs to be cleared for a son or daughter to find their way back safely, without stumbling over the weeds and rubble that have collected on the path of their life over the years.

So, clearance of the path must be done with outstretched hands, as the shepherd waits to see the lost sheep return to walk on a much clearer path, that'll lead them back to the true way given through God's guidelines on the Tablets. For all who return to the ways set down by Him, God reigns forever with justice for all who return in faith to God, from whatever path they've strayed onto over the past years with the enemy. God does give forgiveness and mercy to all who truly repent for their sins against the Father.

God's son paid the ransom for us by dying on the tree, so at this time of year, let us all reflect on it and live by His ways of goodness and love. I'm with you always, even unto the end and beyond the veil, so allow my peace to be with you more each day. Pray to be set free in Jesus' name from any aliments you're suffering with and don't give up.

When the thorns pierced into His head with pain, He didn't cry out! Abide in me and I'll be true to my word and not desert you. Rain lashed down and the blood ran freely from the Son of God, who was born and made man to suffer on the tree to die, then to rise again as torrents of tears flowed unto those who worship God's Son.

He was sent like a lamb to the slaughter for the sins of mankind, to suffer on the tree for us. Weep for our majesty and sing praises of worship to glorify and honour his name. He was a valiant noble king of universal love, who gave hope and mercy unto all he met throughout his journey of life. Follow the call from the mighty shepherd, when he calls us, his sheep, to follow his path to the pasture. Gaze upon his wonders and rejoice in his love, and speak of his teachings which hold truth and wisdom from heaven above, which is the nature of God.

He brings everlasting blessings to all those who follow with faith. May my peace be upon you throughout all your trials of life, for you to seek and find your holy grail of deliverance. May your footsteps guide you to follow with grace and ongoing knowledge the truth of the teaching ways of Christ Jesus the man.

Whose God incarnate, sent to do the Father's work upon earth with you, to set people free who are being held by any type of bondage by vices or sins back to the path safely and to a normal existence. As the Holy Spirit descends upon you through the guidance of our Lord, He wants you, Irene, to teach his ways, as you've walked too long in the shadow of death, and now you must be set free with the rest of God's children, who are still being held victims. You're all being loosened by God's power, so the day will dawn when God's people will be set free from their chains of bondage.

Repent for your sins, and let a father take his daughter or son back into his heart. Where he can guard you, as he is a jealous father who loves all of his children very much, and won't allow them to be taken away from him by the enemy. My people, regain faith in me; I'll never fail to help you. My blessings and peace will dissolve the darkness from your souls, allow this to happen and flow freely into your bodies with the stream of life. God hasn't forsaken you and never will; he's remained faithfully watching over his flock. 'Please believe I'm helping you, Irene, as we are two of a kind in our ways, and both of us say what is on our tongues, that's how we're both true, not false. God put us in the world so.

Here ends the message.

39
God Chooses Messengers

I've given these messages to you in accordance with God's power for the world to have and enjoy. Peace often cannot be gained because of non-forgiveness by many countries around the world and by individuals who must learn to forgive each other. As Jesus taught people to be at peace with each other, so may my words you're writing for the messages, Irene, must be taught by living them and learning with an open mind to change one's life style for the better.

This is the plan that God wants repeated through the messages for his people, so they can learn to walk on the path of righteousness and grow in understanding. These messages are an updated version, using your demonisation many times in the way I teach, which can help people to recall as a reminder. I want you to reach out to as many churches as you can and to deliver my teaching way I've given them to you, as I know you'll do your best to do this for me. Many of my original ways of teaching have been changed so much over time that I can't recognize what some of the laws have turned into, which were passed down by the prophets.

Have faith my people, and you'll soon be set free from whatever ailments you might be suffering with. Believe God loves you and his love will take away all fear and sickness from your body. Remember you might have Demon strongholds giving you human suffering as it gives them a sadistic pleasure. I want you and other people who might be victims to start changing your thought patterns into believing that miracles can take place and do happen. See happier times coming for all those being held in any type of bondage in the near future and in the years ahead. Start to believe in God's power, and many great things will come to pass for all who are suffering.

I'm using Irene as an example who has a steadfast spirit of goodness within her which is endearing, and that the devils can never change or take away from her. You're mine to the end and beyond, and you'll never know the reason why you belong to me. Who am I? Perhaps you'll never learn or understand why I'm with you through all your anguish and pain, but I know you're on the road to salvation. This is a truly wonderful path to be on, as your type of journey was once taken by our Lord a long time ago during his time on earth. Let him be a guiding light for you to follow and in the ways of always being merciful to other people, and mercy shall be given unto you until your journey of life comes to an end.

I don't want people suffering; I want them to gain the truth and the way to follow their true calling, which is sent through the Holy Spirit to very few people by the Father. You must follow what you feel is the right way of living for you while you're on the earth and not let the enemy take your body, mind, or soul. It's a long battle from the darkness into the light, and the journey can be a long and tiring one. But if you're steadfast, you'll see rays of light appearing when you least expect them. Always seek the right path to the end of your journey and change path if you're misled onto the wrong one. Demonic spirits are trapped in their own darkness and their hatred of God, who represents true love.

As the light begins to cover the darkness, it will gradually fade away and become non-existent. Believe me, if any of you have demons living in God's temple, they must get out. They come to destroy and defy God's laws by residing within your body, and are committing a crime that must come to an abrupt end by God's hand, and by whom He chooses to end this ordeal.

40
Guidance

Praise the words of the Lord, and give thanks unto our God, whose teachings Christians abide by. He drank the cup as an example for mankind and laid a path to follow. That's why God chooses people who believe in Him to do His work on earth.

These types of people have faith, and things will change for them if they are suffering from various kinds of ailments. Many people are living with horrendous ordeals of suffering in their lives, are weary and tired of ongoing sickness, and have prayed endlessly for God's help. They seek to be delivered from the demons of sickness that create ailments against many Christians for their religion, making them wonder what Christ is doing to help or stop their suffering.

In the world, there are many extraordinary cases of people being plagued with illness that might be caused by different vices they've picked up from demons attached to their lives. These types of connections can drive people to an early grave. Satan is still busy at work in the world we all live in, creating evil beyond one's imagination, to pervert and corrupt humankind on earth.

People's journey of life can be one with constant trials and a weary one that drains daily life and energy, which can happen to any Christian when the enemy aims to destroy their lives. So, be aware of this unseen enemy of the human race.

Have faith and trust in God, pray for yourself and other people who are suffering with mental or physical problems for them to be healed.

41
Life Journey

The road is long and forever changing over time, so let it be altered gradually to transform the hearts of the people on earth. This way, they will know and understand that God is still alive and can be in touch with the earth; He is not a distant image who has gone and separated from the world. God still abides in many churches, looking down and seeing where His word is being preached and where the teaching of the word is not being understood due to the way it is taught today. Christ Jesus taught in a very simple way, often using parables in most of His teachings.

Some people follow Christianity as it's presented by a priest or through family traditions, but sometimes these people are misguided by the way the words are preached and can become fanatical in their interpretation of my word, which can cause people to lose faith in me. These types of people are not of my blood or the family of God, as they have not been born again through true baptism by the Holy Spirit.

The Holy Spirit is poured out on many people or a person when their nature is truly pleasing to God, not merely by the teachings given out by many churches. If the church hasn't been able to resolve your problem, Jesus can help your deliverance from suffering that takes place gradually.

The Holyland's roots were planted deep and can't be uprooted by pressures of the world, and patience's a virtue to attain.

42
God's Solutions

God's omnipotent love is evident in saying, 'loving one's brothers and sisters on the journey of life,' as we draw from a pool of love and faith that God instils in each person in the world. If my children choose to draw strength from the pool of life, it's their own choice. The human race is given free will from birth to choose by God, who is always waiting for His children to turn to Him like a father for help when we cannot find a solution to our problems quickly enough. Often, it can take a lifetime to find the answers we seek on earth.

But God can always find a way, although sometimes not quickly, as in your case, Irene. Remember, that enemy comes in many different disguises and forms while we continue searching for answers. Whether we call him the Devil, Satan, or by any other name, how can the father of lies resolve my people's lives when they all belong to me?

As their father, I hold the answers to most of their lifelong issues, and I understand why they have them. When the devil enters a person's body, he uses their life force as his host to search for any weaknesses they might have, intending to use these against them later. Over time, the body becomes a self-destructive force, using its own energy to abuse itself, driven by the enemy's torments and abuse, eventually leading to the body's destruction. If the enemy continues residing inside or attached to a victim, using up their energy and causing illness, will lead to the body's destruction. This vile attack will continue until a form of intervention comes through deliverance to end the situation, which can last for a lengthy time.

43
Be an Example

Blessings on you, my people and Irene. God does love you; never doubt this as you walk His ways. Soon, no enemy will be able to touch you once your ordeal is taken away for good. So, have faith the Lord delivers people and finds ways to heal them. Mighty is God's mercy for all who continue praying for peace in the world and for themselves. It will come to pass by His hand. My people your doubts in the Lord are natural after years of suffering, but God knows you've never stopped searching for an answer, and that pleases Him.

The enemy listens Irene to know what your words are from me to write. Many lives are still being kept on hold by oppression of not being free people. Because of some type of demonization of their body and want their life and body back as they were when they were born, and to regain their lives for the time they have left on earth.

You're mine to the end, and you'll be freed, I repeat, as it's been my life's work on earth for many years to save and uphold many of my people and you from the demonic, unclean spirits that entered their bodies which is unseen. These are parasites of the worst type that inflict torments on people who belongs to me and the Father above. Let your soul take flight in the light of God; his love and power are a wondrous thing that's flowing endlessly into the universe of life on earth.

Your doubts are being given by those attached to you, so you must learn to start removing doubts and stop building more walls that will become harder to break down. I've always been with you in your darkest hours of despair, even when you believed you were alone and lost from me forever. My love has stood the test of God the Father to watch over you and my people on earth. Trust your heart and believe in what you know is right for you, as the wheels of time begin to knock down the walls that have been erected. Don't let people's opinions give you more bricks to rebuild new walls and barriers against your faith.

Christ will bring you all to safety from the storms in your life. Remember my words and teach them to others, as this is what the Father wants done. I will lift you up each time you feel low in your faith, through the enemy, and losing life to breathe in me and live. My blessings to you and all Christians. The enemy, is always at work to destroy people of divine grace with God. Trust in God; He is not doing anything evil to any of you. It's Satan at work in one of God's own, whom He created to obey and live in His ways, to be an example of how life evolves with its trials. Through being born into the human race on earth, may you find the truth you seek with the light of Jesus Christ on your quest, and find the path of everlasting peace.

Peace be with you all

44
Path of Salvation

My crucifixion and suffering were my joy, knowing that you are all on the path of salvation in a truly wonderful way, a path I took once a long ago on earth. Be merciful in how you treat others, and mercy will be given unto you. I don't gain pleasure from any Christian suffering; I want you to know this is the truth. Each person has a calling to achieve in their life, sent by the Father, and each man or woman must do what feels right for them. So, avoid the enemy's wiles to change the course you have chosen for your life, if an attachment of unclean spirits appears to disrupt your path.

Once these perpetrators from the realms of darkness enter your life, over time, they will take away light and happiness. And the return journey from darkness into the light is a tiring and painful one. For anyone, this voyage is arduous, and you must remain steadfast with your goal. Until you see small rays of light appearing over time until you are set free from the bondage which holds you.

The world today is diverse, where many people are living dangerously with various freedoms and lifestyles, which open doors for the realms of spiritual darkness to enter. The younger generation is unaware that their bodies can be easily trapped in a world of spiritual darkness. When this takes place, people can develop a hatred for God, as they become victims of various evil spirits by mixing with the wrong people, and don't realize their lives are heading for disaster.

The world of corruption leads any victim down a path to their own destruction over time, with various crimes, vices, and deeds committed and instigated against God's laws. The realms of darkness are generally in charge when this is happening, with demonic spirits whose goal is to destroy people's lives. The signs are evident, but no one seems to notice what's going on. When this starts taking place in a person's life, their character changes. They listen to gossip, believe the lies they hear, and begin to enjoy watching violent and oppressive acts of sadistic cruelty on TV and in films.

People can be attacked from a supernatural plane daily and have no idea this is happening, as it is unseen. And have no idea you are being mentally attacked on a supernatural level as your interest grows in horror movies. Violent and frightening horror scenes in films can have a devastating effect on us mentally, which we never realize. Also, that spiritual forces of wickedness could be at work through various circumstances in our lives. Next, you're not sleeping well, and your working life becomes hard to endure because you are tired but still stay up late watching horror films.

I do not want to overload whoever is reading this book with my personal views, but we need a basic faith to keep us grounded and on course in our vessel of life. God is the light of the world and says, 'No demon or stronghold can take what belongs to the Father and destroy it, if the child is not willing. I am the light of the world who can bring lasting peace to end your nightmares. Irene, your name translates in Greek as peace; may it be with you.'

Jesus knew the enemies' tactics with what he offered would bring destruction for the world, with corruption and roots of wickedness for humankind to follow. We have free choice so, some people follow what he offers, that leads to a despairing existence of utter misery, death, and suicide if they accept the father of lies and his games with human lives.

Keep the Holy Family in your life with the angels and saints. Roses have thorns, so treasure the graces you have been given and enjoy the world around you, my people. Our Lady was steadfast in her ways, and Jesus showed mercy to those with infirmities. Speak, and he listens to the people who pray to him with faith. The cross is a symbol of life and a restoration of your trust in God. It is a sign of new beginnings to bring health and peace back into your lives in a multitude of ways. My angels and saints are standing guard, praying for everyone to be restored to health, happiness, and my peace. Bless you, daughter.

45
I'm Here to Help

Search for small things in each day that give you pleasure. By doing this, healing can begin to take place, and you'll feel happier. The Lord gives in abundance to people who trust Him, as the joy of giving is greater than receiving. Picture your goal and let God find the way for you to achieve it. Don't fret; you can achieve everything. Nothing is impossible if the goal is the right one. Spread God's name and praise Him to gather more to the flock. By doing this, you're working for the Lord. Peace be with you, my people.

Learn to feel God's strength when He lifts you out of the pits of despair. Regain your strength and hope in your life through His divine love. I know each person's story when they cry out to me, Abba, and hear their cries as I draw close to them. Never doubt me and my love for you and my people. Rejoice; God is always watching over His people who are suffering in despair with their many different issues, and he heals them. God can break the chains that hold people bondage through various illness, and pain. This is a trial that must be dealt with very carefully, that can take time to set a victim completely free. God will release much of the victim's sickness and pain first.

Stand strong on the rock that God will build for you, and He'll send help to free you from your ordeals. Gain trust in me so I can help you all. Silence is golden, and so is peace. I want my people on earth to be closer to me and abide in my love, as my people on earth are my life. I live again through the Father, who is all-powerful and helps people struggling and suffering with the trials of life. I feel and understand each person's pain and agony they want to be delivered from, as the serpent thrives on their suffering.

Tears of pain are like the morning dew as I cry with the long-lost souls who will not repent, and be set free in the name of the Father or in my name. I want to bring freedom to all the lost people by God's almighty power and set lost souls free. Let your mind dwell on thoughts of peace and on the Father in heaven to do this work for you all.

Try saying this each day

I love you, Lord, you are my strength. The Lord is my rock, my fortress, and my deliverer. My God is my rock, in whom I take refuge. He is my shield and the horn of my salvation, my stronghold. I call to the Lord, who is worthy of praise, and I am saved from my enemies. Psalm 18:1-3   Stars never cease to shine their bright silvery beams of light in the sky, and only God can give life and take it away. So, remain with hope for Him to set you free from suffering.

46
Healing and Suffering

No one is destined to suffer by God's will. Instead, God calls for repentance if you've sinned, promising mercy and strength to his people. Have faith that God sends help to alleviate infirmity, pain, and suffering. Sickness can arise from the various fears we live with daily. Therefore, my people, be happier, for this will enable healing to occur more swiftly in your bodies and minds.

I have been told numerous times by religious people, as well by the advocates of lies, that suffering is inevitable. I now understand both perspectives and their meanings. Some claim that God punishes people for their sins, a notion promoted by certain religious figures, while others accept this as a pretext knowing it is the work of the enemy. Recognize that the enemy, is the father of infinite lies and treachery, is tirelessly at work in society to drive people away from churches and make them abandon their faith.

These advocates of destruction are the ones ruining people's lives. They inflict suffering on victims through various forms of torment, and those who endure these trials often never fully recover their health after living with such horrendous conditions. Pray to God for help and he will respond, believe and this will take place gradually.

47
Be the Image of Christ

Our Lord is great; His mercy is endless, and He sends blessings to priests and their parish churches. Learn to open the doors of your churches to let God enter in more fully when He knocks. Don't close the doors to the signs He might be sending to evangelize people for the faith.

To follow Jesus, one must show kindness to those who come asking for help, as you might be the only person they have left to speak with. Never turn people away, which could leave them feeling lost and alone on a road of despair. Whether they have a small problem to discuss or a life-threatening one, you may be their last hope of finding a solution. The key to being a good priest is to make time in your busy day to listen to the people in your parish. By doing this, you're following in Jesus' footsteps, walking the path He took with compassion and understanding for the human race, whom He healed and delivered from various ailments during His ministry.

Never close the doors of your churches to things you might fear or are unable to answer. Every issue has a solution somewhere, and God's knowledge is wider and deeper than the ocean that flows on endlessly. The Lord will give you the answers you need in your moments of silent reflection and prayer, often when you least expect it. Don't create barriers; let people open their hearts and confide in you like a father. By doing this, people can look to you for help and guidance in their times of need. If you follow my words, God's blessings will be with you and the work you do for the Lord in your churches.

Irene has been given these messages to renew faith in people, as the world today is grasping for material things and has forgotten the One who created the earth for humankind to live in. These messages serve as a reminder that God is all-powerful and able to reach out to

Christians on earth through people like Irene. Just as I have done before through various people who have written and spoken about their connections through the Spirit, this is to let people know that God is powerful and watching over the world we live in, and He has the power to touch people on earth, as He has with this book and its messages.

Many of God's children have travelled the earth endlessly, always searching for peace and goodwill, which is a great treasure chest to attain, given by God.

48
How the Messages and Teaching Came

I believe that both *Trials, Torments, and Teachings* and *Messages from Spirit* are being channelled to me through the Holy Spirit from Christ. These messages have been given to me over a lengthy period of suffering that I've experienced for well over fifty years in my life. When this ordeal began in the 1980s, I had no idea or knowledge that I was being demonized by a stronghold of demons. They discovered that I was naturally sensitive, which gave them an open door for easy access to my body and life. Their invasion of my life began during the summer of the 1980s in Ankara, bringing devastating effects that transformed my life and career in show business into a disastrous state. From then onwards, my life was divided into two worlds once the spirits from the realms of darkness attached themselves to my body and life.

The arrival of the teachings came many years later, after a night of being attacked non-stop by unholy spirits, which left me in a traumatic and distressed state. Suddenly, my bedroom filled with a peaceful silence that gradually covered the room and me. Once the silence came, I felt strangely peaceful and didn't know why. I got a pen and some paper and began to write down what I was hearing in my inner mind, and that's how the first teaching was born and written.

From then on, I continued writing down what the unseen power was channelling to me, words that formed in my mind. This continued over the years, appearing to be a form of religious teaching related to what I was suffering. Eventually, I had sufficient teachings to create my first book, *Trials, Torments, & Teachings*. When this book was published, I was still under daily attacks from voices and unclean spirits attached to my body. Being a Christian, I believed that writing my first book was a mission from God, which I had to fulfil to help people improve their lives if they were suffering from similar conditions. Thus, I wrote *Trials, Torments, and Teachings*. This strange supernatural gift that I possessed gave me the power to write my first book. Since then, my knowledge has grown, and I've learned more about the condition that engulfed my body and existence. My advice to Christians is to pick up a copy of the second book I wrote *Haunted by Demons: The Irene Martinez Story* to find out more in-depth information.

This book is another work that's been channelled to me through the Spirit from God, whom I believe exists, though I've been a bit of a doubting Thomas at times. I want whoever reads the messages to form their own opinion about them the proof is in the pudding, so judge for yourselves. Many times, we're blind and fail to recognize God's intervention in our lives. The Savior wants to convey through these messages that He cares for Christian people on earth and is aware of the many trials they bear during their lifetimes.
May peace be with you all.

49
Gods' Intervention

God's intervention often seems slow for those people suffering from long-term illness. However, miracles are happening every day somewhere in the world, even if we are not made aware of them through TV or newspapers. A voice once spoke to me, saying, "Irene, you are one of my living miracles for all to see." There is much more going on in the world around us with things that cannot be seen visually or fully understood, lying close to the world we inhabit.

A thin veil separates us from the other world, a realm filled with silence, peace, and freedom, closer to our existence than a blink of an eye. Very few people comprehend its existence. However, some individuals who have experienced passing through this veil have given their testimonies. These people have all had close encounters with death and describe it as a place of light and peace. Others claim to have spoken to God and angels.

What I encountered in Turkey when I heard voices was not from the heavenly realm, but from a deadly type of energy that gradually took up residence in my life, bringing voices and torment that persisted over the years. My advice is to be vigilant if you start hearing voices from out of nowhere. I ask the person reading these messages to view them with an open mind, as they can bring changes into your life. I believe something extraordinary touched my life after this intervention, something both good and evil, which eventually led to me becoming an author.

God's blessing to you.

50
Discuss God Freely

I'd like you to ask groups of people these questions about the Lord and their faith, encouraging them to seek answers for themselves. Let them explore their faith as you do, to see if they are on the right path to finding their faith and God. By doing this, each person will gain a deeper understanding and faith by applying the laws written in the Bible, which can be used in our daily lives just as they were when Moses received them inscribed on the Tablets.

Let people ask these questions:

1. Do you think Jesus allows people to suffer for a purpose?
2. Is praying helpful with your problems? Does it give you results?
3. Is the Lord similar to a good friend for you?
4. Do you ever pray for lost souls or for people who've died in strange circumstances?
5. Do you pray for the lonely, the sick, or for people living in despairing situations, and for the dying?
6. Do you search to find the truth and answers for your problems?
7. Does Christ Jesus give you hope in your life?
8. How would your life be if you didn't worship God?
9. Do you think sin is a personal choice you make?
10. Which sins do you consider can ruin your life? Let's make a list of things from everyone to discuss sin. Then, think about what can ruin people's lives through vices that appear harmless at first.
11. Where does sin originate from?
12. Do you feel close to God or far away? Ask yourself this question.

13. What does faith mean to you, and do you practice it in your everyday life through your actions?
14. Can you recognize God's creations in the world you live in?
15. Does healing take place through prayer? Have you seen your situations change for the better?
16. What does God represent to you?
17. Is Jesus needed in your life?
18. Do you find the Word of God in the Bible hard to understand, as the world has changed since it was written, even though people's basic needs and ways haven't changed much?
19. Should people be allowed a choice in their religion, or should they stick with what they were brought up with from childhood?
20. Are you interested in gaining more knowledge about Christianity and Jesus?
21. Does the Christian faith help your life?
22. Do you believe that healers, priests, and religious people have the gift to alleviate sickness?
23. Must we have proof of Jesus' survival in the world today?
24. Are we all too busy with our own lives to spend time searching for God's truth?
25. Why is there suffering in the world? What purpose does it serve?
26. Why do problems happen to you? Do you blame God for the catastrophes that strike your life, or do your actions shape your destiny?
27. Are there strange forces at work in the world? Is God leading the good side, while Lucifer waits for us to commit sin and jeopardize our lives?
28. Is prayer needed, and does it help?
29. Why is God forgiving toward us when we stray from the straight and narrow path?
30. Do you believe Christ's sacrifice on the tree takes away sins?
31. Why do people continue sinning today, bringing disastrous consequences for themselves and others?

I want Irene to interpret my messages in a simple way for people to understand the Christian faith as it was taught to my disciples. Please don't pressure people to adopt the Christian religion if they have steadfast beliefs of their own about faith. Allow them to find God in their own way. Let my simple teachings of the Word be a journey of understanding drawn from the world I lived in. I am with you, even though you still doubt my presence, and with everyone in prayer groups. Blessings, good health, and peace to whoever reads my messages, and for you, Irene. Shalom, the Lamb.

51
Plants in the Garden of Life

Irene, what puzzles me is why people in the world we've both lived in, at different times, are still so obsessed with owning many material possessions and living their lives without faith in God, who created the world. Your gift of being a sensitive, with visions, is how I'm able to connect with your inner mind and hear your thoughts. "Who am I?" That's a reasonable question to ask, especially after being tricked by the father of lies into thinking that it was me, which brought devastating effects to your life and health for being a faithful Christian of the Lord.

Many Christians have suffered these types of attacks that you've experienced over the years. These victims also thought God was talking to them. Many religious people have had similar experiences, enduring attacks in their bodies and minds over time from unclean spirits saying, "God wants you to accept this suffering." Then the demon begins attacking the victim continuously, using God's name it's a lie.

This scenario is formed by strongholds of demonic spirits who want a host to live in or be attached to. The Christian victim is then mentally and physically abused for their faith, enduring various torments. God isn't causing these sadistic attacks as a form of penance. Does this help to explain what you've experienced for so long, Irene?

Prayers never go unanswered; the Lord listens and responds in a variety of ways to different people. Trust and pray, and let the living water from heaven flow down upon you, to wash away sickness and heal you. Have faith, for my words are sent to heal my people and you. So, accept the living water in your souls, bodies, and minds to bring peace into your lives. Stand strong on the rock that God will build for you, and the help He sends to free all Christians from their life's trials. Silence is golden, and peace lies within yourself to gain. I want people on earth to be closer to me with their faith and to trust me. My life's work was to serve my children on earth, even when I was taken back to the Father, who is aware of what people are struggling with and suffering through.

When the serpent coils itself around one's life to devour hopes of leading a normal existence, it's when the wrong door opens, allowing the serpent to enter your life. However, this can be undone the chains can be broken to set you free.

Every person is special to God, and He is always waiting to hear your prayers, even though many people doubt my ways. If you have ears, I repeat, listen to your heart; follow where it guides you. There will be a change of heart in the way you think, which will change the whole pattern of your life, laying down a new path for you to follow. Just as plants are reborn each spring after the cold and darkness of winter disappear, plants in the garden of life can be replanted in good soil and can blossom again in God's Garden, a beautiful place. Although each flower is different, they all need sunshine and rain to grow and develop.

Peace, love, and power are being sent to you and my people to bloom each year in my garden. From your friend on high: Bless you all, and keep your thoughts steadfast in remaining faithful to God.

52
The Spirits Journey with Irene

My journey with Irene on earth has been another trial for her, as she tries to understand and interpret my words to write them down as messages. It has also been an experience for me, being close to her connection I will treasure. Irene knew from the beginning of our encounter that many people might not believe what she says is happening to her. They might think she's mentally disturbed if she tells them how the messages came to her. My mission is to spread these messages around the world through this book.

Irene has a connection with me through the spirit and will start working on more books for me through the Holy Spirit, once this book is published. I chose Irene because of her sensitivity to hear my words is a gift from God. She also has the clarity to see visions and predict various events before they happen. Irene has lived many times on earth but never fully understood God's purpose for her. God didn't send unclean spirits to demonize her or cause the suffering she has experienced in the past years.

God knew about the trials she faced with demonization and the battles she bravely fought against evil and corruption. This made her the ideal candidate to spread my words on earth. Her vibrant personality, combined with her long experience working in show business and with the public, makes her adaptable to situations that might arise. That's why the decision was made for Irene to be my messenger to spread the word of God, a difficult task that I have faith she can achieve.

Many people will have doubts about what she says, including many churches that won't believe what she claims comes from the Holy Spirit, who abides in all of us. But with God's blessing and anointing on her journey with my words, I know she'll do her best to spread my messages in her own country first, and then around the world through this book. By participating in God's work on earth and telling the truth about her own experiences, she will testify that the enemy is still active and working tirelessly on earth. This is a true testimony of what can happen in a person's life.

My journey with Irene has been a great experience for me, as I have been able to connect with a person on earth in this way. While I am close to all my people when they pray to me, Irene's sensitivity made it easier to connect with her. I am with most people throughout their journey of life, from their first breath to their last.

Being with Irene has brought back many happy memories of my time on earth with my family. Despite her failing health, she continues to fulfil her daily responsibilities for her son and herself. God will choose those who work with her to bring peace and happiness back into her life. God is merciful and compassionate toward His people.

My love is everlasting, flowing like an ocean with mercy and love for my people. When they ask for help and repent of their sins, that's all God asks. He remains near each person, ready to be with them throughout their journey of life, if they choose to let Him.

Irene has become like a disciple, as I give her my words through the Spirit to write. I have adapted my way of teaching with parables during our many journeys together. Irene has learned to understand my words, their meanings, and my manner of teaching, which is rare. This has been difficult for both of us at times, but we have learned to adjust to each other to achieve the Father's work. I strive to explain exactly what I want to say to her, and she remains patient with me, even while suffering from her own health issues. Yet, she has continued writing persistently over time to complete the messages.
Irene has found the experience of being with me constantly to be unbelievable, something she cannot discuss with anyone, as she would be considered mentally disturbed. This has happened to many

of the people I wish to speak with through the Spirit about doing God's work on earth. They, like Irene, have suffered similar experiences.

Many Christians will find it hard to believe that I am actually with her and speak to her daily. She is a normal, logical person who suddenly found me in her reality of life some years ago, giving her teachings from out of nowhere. So, she has never been fully convinced that I am with her as her Savior. Irene is a sensitive with the power to see visions and hear the Spirit, but our connection is different from what psychic people hear. This is difficult for anyone to grasp, especially those who have suffered from the enemy's attacks.

Irene is delivering these messages as a loyal Christian who still believes in God despite years of suffering. She has been used as a scapegoat for religion by the enemy, trying to convert the one person who doesn't want to be converted by the father of lies. She's a tough cookie, as they say in America!

After hearing various voices and having horrific experiences, it's normal to ask, "Who are you? What do you want?" Finally, she is understanding that her role is to be a messenger for me. Although she still has doubts about me, there's a bit of Thomas in her, like one of my disciples.

I hope Irene will gradually have faith and trust in me, as I do love her very much. We have so much in common in our ways and thoughts. She will always belong to me and the Father. I hope my words, conveyed through her, will be accepted by my people on earth and that they will be of use and learned. I want my journey on earth with Irene to be remembered, as it was special for me.

I hope everyone who hears about our journey together and reads the messages in this book will find lasting hope in them. I want people to gain a deeper understanding of how powerful God is and how He can be in their lives. I am showing my power through Irene, whom I chose to be with on earth and use as my messenger to spread my messages. I have done this many times before with visitations of different types to the people I choose, as does my mother with her visitations to many different countries in the world. I hope Irene will plant good seeds in people's hearts and minds for me that will continue to grow throughout the years on earth.

I hope that in time, Irene and I will become a joint team in our efforts to bring the word of God back to the people through these books. People on earth need to regain a deeper closeness to God in their world, which today is full of strife and destruction. As people seem to be seeking self-gratification, power, and greed, they open doors to let the power of evil enter their hearts and minds, affecting their lives and judgment. We need to return to God's values to live happier lives as His people on earth.

If we start working together for a better future with peace and harmony in our lives and in the world, this can help people make positive changes in their lives and create a chain reaction, bringing the value of the tablets back into fashion on earth. I pray that this will happen through these messages and that more harmony will evolve around the world. This can also help each individual person on their journey throughout life on earth.

By the power of God's will, it will take place, as He loves his children and wants them to be free from illness, pain, and suffering, which might be brought about by the hands of the enemy if he crosses a person's path during their lifetime. Many people have faced endless trials, and only God knows why. He is the only one who can set you all free from whatever you're suffering with. Trust, never doubt, and learn to believe in God, who made creation, and believe in the love of Christ.

Recollections of My Story

I'm Irene Martinez, the author of the book you're reading, *Messages from Spirit*. My journey to writing my first book, *Trials, Torments, and Teachings*, began through the events that took place in my life starting in the 1980s, when I was working in Turkey as a singer, dancer, and fully trained entertainer. At that time, I had no idea that I was a sensitive, or what the public usually calls a medium, with abilities like clairvoyance, clairaudience, and the power to see visions. So, when I started hearing voices one evening in my hotel room, I didn't know what was happening or where the voices were coming from.

I checked the corridor of the hotel to see if anyone had a radio or cassette playing, but it was silent. From the moment I heard the voices, my life gradually changed into one of chaos. I was a fit person when this issue began, doing one-hour nonstop shows and long rehearsals daily. Suddenly, I couldn't sleep and was experiencing strange, out-of-the-ordinary events daily in my work and at the hotel. I was always a Christian and often thought that it was God speaking to me. However, I now know it was the enemy using a Christian as a scapegoat to abuse and manipulate, along with other unclean spirits.

I returned to England, leaving my show in Turkey behind. My long marriage broke up, as did my career in show business. I visited various churches, but the condition didn't end. The voices continued and attached themselves to me. This is a horrific condition for anyone to live with having your life haunted by spirits from the realms of darkness.

This torment has lasted for well over fifty years. Some years later, I began writing down my experiences and what had been happening to me since my nightmare began in Turkey. That's when I felt an overwhelming sense that the Holy Spirit might have touched my life somehow. Through suffering with this unholy condition that plagued my life, I gradually understood that my faith might have been sustaining me. I self-published my book *Trials, Torments & Teachings* in 2015.

My second book, *Haunted by Demons: The Irene Martinez Story*, gives you an inside look into my life, living with the strange supernatural condition of demonization that began in Turkey in the 1980s. This condition, which is still affecting people around the world today, is not a myth but a devastating reality of living with spirits of the worst kind from the realms of darkness. I'm a Christian and have faith in God. I still believe that the Lord will help you with whatever you're suffering from in your life. After more than fifty years of horrendous, unseen suffering that only my family and church know about, I share my story.

I know there'll be many sceptics who will argue, discuss, and dismiss my story people who won't believe or understand what I've been living with daily for many years. This can happen to anyone, as it did to me, bringing havoc both physically and mentally. It's a living hell, being terrorized, abused, and tormented endlessly for years, a victim of a type of bondage that clings to your body and life. It is a never-ending horror story. This condition exists I've experienced it. If you have any questions, know this: God exists, and so do demons.

In the Bible, you read stories about possession and how Jesus Christ cast demons out of people's bodies during His ministry on earth. Many of these infirmities were caused by unclean spirits attached to people's bodies. Christ Jesus was an exorcist and healer who set people free from evil spirits and healed them from many different infirmities of the body and mind caused by demonization. His ministry brought the word of God to the people, starting Christianity, which changed the course of history.

Healing and exorcism were later passed down to His disciples through God as gifts for mankind, to set them free from illness, pain, and suffering that plagued the earth in Jesus's time. The work that Jesus started was continued by His disciples and has continued to the present through the spreading of the Gospels throughout the world. God's plan was accomplished through the resurrection of Christ Jesus on the Cross, which brought the ultimate proof of life after death.

I hope this book has brought you comfort and guidance in your daily life. May you recognise the loving presence of God, who is ever active in the world and walks with you on your journey.

With Prayers, Peace and Blessings

Irene Martinez

www.ingramcontent.com/pod-product-compliance
Lightning Source LLC
Chambersburg PA
CBHW071300040426
42444CB00009B/1799